Della

MW01037178

THE POWER OF WORDS

UNLOCK YOUR ABILITY TO LEARN AND DO ANYTHING

www.strangepowerofwords.com

WATERBURY
PUBLISHERS
www.waterburypublishers.com

Written by Sean Clouden

Cover design by Mario Kroes and Sarah Clouden

Illustrations by Alex Scott

First Edition

Printed in Canada

"You must read *The Power of Words*! You need to get it if you want to control your future and take advantage of the KNOWLEDGE available to all of us. Your future success is only limited to the amount of action you take, and the amount of action you take is only limited to how secure you are in what you understand. I recommend this simple and easy to read book by Sean Clouden. I use the content every day to make decisions and take action."

—Grant Cardone
Sales expert and author

"If you invest the short time it takes to read, understand and apply the basic principles in this book, there is little doubt you will be a much bigger success than you otherwise would have been. There truly is POWER in words . . . ."

—Doug Dohring
Founder of Neopets.com and CEO of The Dohring Company

"As a best selling author I can attribute my success to understanding the power of words. This book should be in the hands of every child and every parent, for the information can change the cousre of cultures and lead Mankind into a much brighter, happier world. Don't believe me? Read *The Power of Words* and you'll see!"

—Tony Melvin
Author of *From Red to Black: How to Get Out of Debt*

"Words are the building blocks of communication, understanding, and life. Creative thoughts and illusions are prerequisites for effective actions, which are the cornerstones of the competence and abilities that bring about happiness and wealth.

"This book presents the most robust explanation of the power of understanding words, as they determine the sphere of one's thoughts, illusions, and actions."

—Dr. Rubik Atamian
Associate Professor of Accounting at The University of Texas Pan-American

"I'm more excited about learning and reading and expanding my vocabulary than I thought possible. When I saw the title of the book I thought I knew what I was in for. I was so wrong! This book brings together incredible data from many authors, philosophers, and historians on the subject of words and just how powerful they really are and why. I want more! After this read I am definitely looking further into this!"

—Joy Gendusa
CEO of PostcardMania, Inc. and Inc. 500 recipient

"Good communication is the key to building a successful business and words are the key to good communication. Sean Clouden gets it right in *The Power of Words*."

—Richard Haddrill
CEO of Bally Technologies, Inc.

"*The Power of Words* was an incredible learning experience for me. As a co-owner of a management training company I have seen first-hand how a client can get hung up on a word or words and seemingly paralyze right there. We would find his ability to apply what he had learned had slowed or stopped. Hours are sometimes spent trying to get the client to be able to "figure out" what he was studying so that he can apply his training. By using the data in *The Power of Words,* my staff can now quickly identify precisely what word or term he did not fully understand, clear it up and magically he can now apply what he has learned. The client is happy, his organization expands and he too recognizes *The Power of Words.* Thank you so much for this simple and powerful book."

—Shaun Kirk
Co-Founder of Measurable Solutions, Inc.

∾ Dedication ∾

This book is dedicated to the great thinkers who knew that the simplest truths are sometimes the greatest and who never forgot to consider the small things.

❧ Acknowledgements ☙

Thank you mom and dad for all of your support, and thank you Sarah for your undying patience and understanding.

Thanks are also due to Sonya, Mario, Kiersten, and Lisa. This project wouldn't be possible without your help.

"The beginning of wisdom is a definition of terms."

—Socrates

CONTENTS

IMPORTANT NOTE

In the back of this book you will find an extensive glossary that contains many commonly misunderstood terms. It is there to aid you in understanding this book, so please use it!

INTRODUCTION

The greatest minds in history have known about and used the power of words to illuminate the world. Every advance of knowledge and every great movement that have become footprints in our history began in the same humble way: as an idea flashing before someone's eyes.

Through the power of words, these ideas, so beautifully expressed, were given lives of their own. From their birthplace in one person's mind, words enabled them to travel the globe, endure the centuries, and influence the way we view ourselves, our fellows, and our existence as a whole.

Leonardo da Vinci's words gave us revolutionary insights in the fields of science, mathematics, art, and engineering, and they revealed a mind still considered superhuman almost 500 years after his death.

Shakespeare wove words into some of the most legendary stories ever told, sparking a literary revolution that not only expanded the world of drama and poetry, but the English language itself.

Sir Isaac Newton's words have proven to be some of the most influential in humankind's history: they became sacred laws of science that changed the way we understand the universe.

Through the power of words, these people and their ideas have been granted immortality.

But most of us don't understand the incredible power of words. Words have the power to unlock the full potential of your intelligence, success, and ability in any area of your life. But ignoring the power of words can lead you to stupidity, failure, and disability.

We live in a Golden Age of Knowledge but a Dark Age of Learning Abilities. We've accumulated so much knowledge of life but so little about how to best learn it. We've turned to science to solve our learning difficulties, but all that's gotten us is complex theories about the brain, psychiatric labels, and dangerous, mind-altering drugs.

As you will soon see, the same great geniuses who built the foundation of this Golden Age of Knowledge also gave us the blueprint for the Golden Age of Learning Abilities. All we have to do is follow it.

This book is going to show you exactly how to follow this blueprint, and it will take you on a journey of understanding the roots of knowledge, wisdom, and ability. By the end, you will not only understand the incredible power of words, but you will also take away an easy-to-use, precise system that will unlock your ability to learn and do anything.

So let's get started.

Chapter One

THE MAGIC WINDOW

"The will to win, the desire to succeed, the urge to reach your full potential . . . these are the keys that will unlock the door to personal excellence."
—Confucius, deeply influential Chinese philosopher

What if you had a magic window?

Whenever you look through your magic window, everything that was once confusing becomes simple. Everything that is complicated or tough to understand becomes a breeze.

If you could look into the business world through such a window, how long would it take you to build an empire?

What would you use the window for? Think about this. Would you become a business mogul? Would you become an incredible artist? Maybe you'd get a degree?

Imagine it. Like a strong wind blowing away clouds, all false ideas and theories would vanish. All uncertainty would disappear, and all that would remain is a clear sunbeam of confidence, truth, and simplicity.

Galileo once wrote, "All truths are easy to understand once they are discovered; the point is to discover them." What if you could quickly and easily discover truths in any field or activity?

In short, you would be *unstoppable*, wouldn't you?

Once you understand the simple concepts this book is about to reveal, you will have such a window for *any* activity in life. Business,

1

school, relationships, hobbies—anything.

Business. School. Relationships. Hobbies. Anything.

Sounds impossible, right?

Well, you don't have to believe it yet, but by the end of this book, you will.

Read on.

Chapter Two

THE SECRET YOU DIDN'T REALIZE YOU KNEW

"Being ignorant is not so much a shame, as being unwilling to learn."
—Benjamin Franklin, one of the Founding Fathers of the United States

When you were a child, can you remember how exciting it was to learn new things? Remember your feeling of success and accomplishment that came with riding a bike for the first time, learning to swim, and playing your first sport? Life was great, wasn't it?

Do you still feel the same excitement toward life? Do you still wake up every day just itching to get started? If not, what do you think it would take to revive those feelings?

Well, you will soon discover how you can restore that power and keep it forever!

You may not realize it yet, but your childhood actually holds the secret to your competence, intelligence, success, and happiness. You learned this lesson early, but you probably didn't recognize it for what it was—the playbook for leading a truly fulfilling and great life.

Yes, the playing field has changed—you've gone from the old neighborhood to the "real world"—but the rules are actually the same.

American oil baron Henry L. Doherty once said, "Get over the idea that only children should spend their time in study. Be a student so long as you still have something to learn, and this will mean all your life."

Keep in mind, Henry left school at age twelve to work at the Columbia Gas Company. He aggressively educated himself, and by his eighth year at the company, he had risen to the position of chief engineer. Soon after, he started his own company; by his mid-twenties, he had already begun building his empire—an empire that would ultimately include more than two hundred companies, mainly consisting of utilities and oil refineries.

So, what is the secret to recapturing all these wonderful feelings we had as a child?

Would you believe the answer actually lies in *studying*? How could that be?

Well, let's look at this. Why should anyone bother studying? Because you need to pass an exam? To get a degree? To sound smart? None of these things are the *real* reason why you should study.

Years ago, a good friend of mine, a business professor at a prestigious university, shared an insightful statement with me about studying. He said if you spent an hour or two every day studying any field you are actively involved in, within two to three years, you'd be in the top 1 to 5 percent of that field. He came to that conclusion after many years of meeting, talking with, and reading about successful people. He found many of these people were self-taught, and all were die-hard students of their fields.

They were always learning something new; they never felt they knew it all. More importantly, however, they were able to *apply* what they learned.

Years ago, a university conducted a study that delved into the factors of success. The researchers analyzed salespeople who were earning more than $250,000 per year in sales, and they considered many different aspects of these people. After much research, however, they found these successful people had *one* key thing in common. What was it?

Speed of implementation.

What is "speed of implementation"? Well, it's simply the time

between the moment you hear or learn about something and the moment you *put it into action*.

This study found that these successful people would get an idea and *immediately* put it in action to find out whether it worked. They were fanatical with their speed of implementation, and they made a lot of money operating this way.

As Thomas Edison once said, "The value of an idea lies in the using of it."

What I'm getting at here is successful people waste no time in *doing things*. They take swift, effective action and get results because of it.

In his dictionary of 1828, Noah Webster wrote that "to study" means "to apply the mind to; to read and examine for the purpose of learning and understanding."

Before you are able to *do* anything competently, you must learn about it and understand it. As you probably know, the only way to learn and understand things is to study them. Aristippus, a Greek philosopher and student of Socrates, said that "native ability without education is like a tree without fruit."

Unfortunately, getting fruit to grow in our mental tree can sometimes be frustratingly hard. We've all experienced this before. You can surely remember times where you failed to successfully learn and do something.

But what if you were so good at studying you could learn and understand *anything*, and then be able to *immediately* do it? Imagine if you could take anything you're already good at and rapidly accelerate your skills through simple study?

Wouldn't it be amazing if you knew, with confidence, that you could *do* anything because of your ability to quickly learn about and understand it?

What would you learn?

What would you do?

This book will teach you an incredibly simple yet ingenious method of study that will give you just that ability.

The legendary writer and philosopher Francis Bacon once said that "natural abilities are like natural plants—they need pruning by study." I'm going to show you how to plant the seeds of ability and then grow and prune them into a stunning landscape of competence and intelligence that will leave people in *awe*.

What I'm about to reveal isn't speed reading. It has nothing to do with memory tricks. You can apply it entirely on your own to *any* subject, and it has been around for over thirty years. Millions of people from every walk of life already use this fascinating method every day, yet chances are, you've never seen anything like it.

And it all begins with the simplest of things . . . *words*.

Chapter Three

THE STRANGE POWER OF WORDS

"Words are some of the most powerful and important things I know . . . Language is the tool of love and the weapon of hatred. It's the bright red warning flag of danger—and the stone foundation of diplomacy and peace."
—*Unknown*

There once was a man named Johnson O'Connor. O'Connor was a Harvard graduate who spent his early years researching astronomical mathematics under the famous astronomer Percival Lowell. In the 1920s, General Electric hired O'Connor to study and test its successful employees and discover which traits they had in common that made them good at their jobs. The company wanted to be able to test new employees and, based on the results, assign them to jobs that best fit their personalities and skills. This research and experimentation was the beginning of O'Connor's lifelong journey: the study of human talents and learning.

To expand his research efforts, in 1930, he founded the Human Engineering Laboratory at the Stevens Institute of Technology. O'Connor gathered data on skills specific to various professions, but he also gathered general data regarding abilities and learning. He launched a research project to determine whether certain talents were more important than others in becoming successful and advancing in one's career. It was during this testing that he made an unexpected discovery.

He found a person's *vocabulary level* was the *best single predictor* of success in *any area*. In other words, an understanding of not only general language but of the words specific to the activity was the most important factor that separated the unsuccessful from the successful!

This discovery began O'Connor's fascination with language and its connection with ability and success. In another study, O'Connor found a person's vocabulary directly correlated with how far that person rose in an organization. Presidents of companies scored among the highest in vocabulary of those people he tested.

In his later writings, O'Connor concluded the understanding of words was a *major key* to unlocking human potential.

Why is this so? According to O'Connor, the answer seems to be that words are the tools with which we think and with which we grasp others' thoughts. O'Connor fiercely opposed those educators who believed only the *usage* of words mattered and that standard, precise definitions, such as those found in a dictionary, were irrelevant. "We can't let the ignorant define our words for us," he argued.

Many other influential men and women have written about the power of words. Famous author Rudyard Kipling once said, "Words are, of course, the most powerful drug used by mankind." Philosopher Jean-Paul Sartre described words as "loaded pistols." Over 100 years ago, Edgar Allan Poe even wrote a short story called "The Power of Words."

"Words have set whole nations in motion and upheaved the dry hard ground on which rests our social fabric," wrote the great novelist Joseph Conrad. "Give me the right word and the right accent and I will move the world." But do most of us value words the way these people did? Probably not. Most of us think the only reason to know words is to have a good vocabulary so we can sound intelligent or score well on tests, right?

What gives? Did these writers and philosophers know something we don't? Just how powerful are words?

Would you believe your inability to learn or to do anything has only to do with you not understanding words?

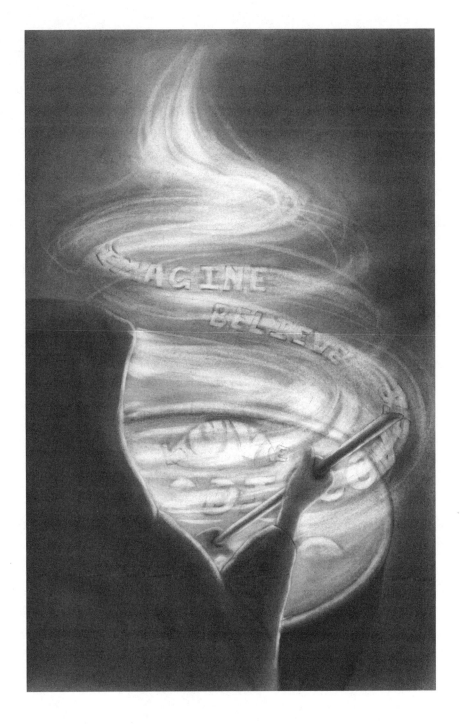

What if misunderstood words are the prime factor in stupidity and are at the bottom of all confusion?

Would you believe if you understood every word you read, you'd be able to immediately apply what you have learned and get results?

As you will soon see, those statements are dead-on. It sounds outrageous, right? I can hear your mind saying, "no way . . . how could that be?"

Well, let's take a look at this.

We're going to do an exercise here that illustrates the importance of knowing words when trying to do things. We're going to paint a picture in our minds.

1. Paint a picture of a house.

2. Paint a fence around the house.

3. Paint a bird flying over the house.

4. Now paint a dub in the front yard.

Have you done that yet? No? Do it. Paint a dub.

Why can't you do it? What happened?

You probably don't know what a *dub* is, do you? Well, *dub* is a Scottish word for a pond.

So, paint a dub in the front yard.

Now you could do it, couldn't you?

Though simple, this example is very effective in showing what happens when you don't understand a word. Nothing drains the wind from the sails of your ability to do something faster than misunderstood words.

When you want to learn how to do something, you must understand certain things about it. The hows and whys. The dos and don'ts. You must understand these things *conceptually*; if you merely memorize words but have no true understanding of them, you may pass tests, but you won't be able to build machines.

Remember, words represent concepts and things. A *concept* is an idea of something formed in the mind. One has the concept, for instance, that another person is tired, that people are bored, or that someone feels sorry for themself. Thought and emotion both are included in concepts. Let's do a quick exercise in conceptual understanding.

Think of a picture of the inside of your car. Look at the steering wheel, the gear shift, the pedals. Good. Those are pictures you are looking at—that isn't conceptual understanding.

Now get the idea of how you drive the car. Get the idea of how it feels to coordinate the gas, brake and clutch pedals and use the gear shift. Did you have to think of a bunch of pictures to do this? No, you just *know* how it feels. That's conceptual understanding.

If you ever learned to play an instrument, this should make immediate sense to you. Can you remember in the beginning when you had to visualize the instrument and think about where to place your hands in order to play the music?

And then as you got better, your hands almost knew exactly where to go on their own. You gained a conceptual understanding of how to do it and just *acted*.

Let's relate this to words. Get a picture of an angry person. Look at his or her face and posture.

Now get the idea of the feeling of anger. What is that emotion like?

See the difference?

Simply memorizing things doesn't give you a conceptual understanding, either. Sure, you could conceptually understand something and memorize the words used to communicate it if you wanted, but can you remember a time—maybe in school—where you memorized something but had no *real* understanding of it? Sure, you could parrot off the words but they didn't add up to any sort of clear idea in your mind. You probably couldn't really think with the information and use it, could you?

Realize that words mean nothing on their own. They are simply vehicles for expressing ideas, feelings, and experiences. If we were all telepathic, life would be much easier—you'd simply beam your concepts and the person receiving them would immediately and fully understand your thoughts, feelings, pictures, and so on.

Unfortunately, it's not that easy. But there's a solution: words. Words are the symbols we use to represent our reality. When you read something, you're observing into someone else's world; if you want to fully understand it like you understand your own, you'd better fully understand the words that person is using to describe it.

When you're trying to learn and do something, you have two options: you can try to figure it all out on your own—observing, thinking, and testing—or you can take a shortcut and have someone who has worked it out explain things to you, whether in person or through a book. Either way, as you know, you have to *study* something before you can *do* it.

If you're studying and don't understand various words, you won't *correctly* understand the sentences. If you don't *correctly* understand sentences, you won't *correctly* understand paragraphs. If you don't *correctly* understand paragraphs, you won't *correctly* understand pages.

By the end of studying a book in which you found many misunderstood words, who knows what you would and wouldn't understand. You'd have a drastically different view of the subject or activity than the author—the person who is trying to communicate to you the attitudes, ideas, and actions that he or she has found beneficial or successful.

A good analogy for this would be shooting a bow and arrow. If you're going to try and hit a bulls-eye fifty feet away, you're going to need to launch the arrow with perfect precision—with just enough force and at just the right angle. If you are off by a few inches of pull or by a degree or two of angle, you could end up missing the target by many feet.

When you're trying to learn something, the "bulls-eye" of study is full conceptual understanding with *no* confusion and the ability to immediately *do* it.

Understanding the words is the same as precisely aiming the arrow. If you fully understand the words—if your arrow is perfectly aimed—you'll nail the bulls-eye and fully understand the concepts being communicated. The ability to do follows naturally.

If you don't understand words—if your aim is bad—you'll miss the target completely and end up with weird ideas and problems doing anything with them.

Herbert Spencer, the English philosopher who coined the phrase "survival of the fittest" in the 1800s, said, "How often misused words generate misleading thoughts." And how right he was.

Now, you may be already thinking, "learning words . . . how boring does that sound?" Yes, I'll admit, it doesn't sound very glamorous. But trust me, it is effective. It's like working out. Toiling away in the gym every day isn't an appealing activity, but having high alertness and energy levels and seeing a toned body staring back at you in the mirror every day is, right? Well, the methods revealed in this book tone your mind and actually make it fun.

So, how do you unlock the power of words?

Don't worry; it's not as hard as you might think. It might seem difficult at first, but as you practice what you learn here, the entire process will become easier and easier. And then, one day, it'll just become second nature to you.

In his two-volume work, *Six Blind Elephants*, Steve Andreas wrote, "It is one thing to realize that the beginning stages of learning are often inevitably difficult and uncomfortable. It is quite another to use that discomfort as a reason not to learn anything new."

So keep an open mind, and just relax and read. I'll make the learning process easy for you.

Chapter Four

THE ONLY WAY TO BECOME A GENIUS

"Continuous effort—not strength or intelligence—is the key to unlocking our potential."
—Winston Churchill, former Prime Minister of the United Kingdom

The famous archaeology journalist C.W. Ceram once said genius "is the ability to reduce the complicated to the simple." How true and how fitting that definition is for what I'm about to show you.

If you were a genius, how do you think that would affect your life? Stop and think about it for a second. Would you help others? Would you use your abilities to make more money? How much do you suppose you could make? Would you improve your health? Would you achieve some kind of desirable status or position?

What if you actually looked forward to studying because you positively *knew* it was going to increase your ability and knowledge, and you would use that growth to create real results? What if you absolutely knew your study guaranteed you would improve in your business, hobbies, relationships, education . . . in *anything*?

F. Scott Fitzgerald, one of the twentieth century's greatest writers, said genius "is the ability to put into effect what is on your mind." Sounds so simple, doesn't it?

Imagine that every time you walk into a bookstore, you feel a rush of excitement because you know you're in a goldmine just overflowing with treasure. You know thousands of years of wisdom is at your fingertips, and you're one of the few who can—and will—use it to achieve success, wealth, knowledge, and ability.

Well, my friend, that *is* the truth of the matter, and the golden bridge to this fantasy is built by *learning words.*

Antisthenes, a Greek philosopher and student of Socrates, wrote that "the investigation of the meaning of words is the beginning of education."

But how do you investigate the meaning of words in such a way that you can learn and do anything? Most of us are taught to try to figure out the meaning of words by looking at their context. This is sloppy, at best, and usually leads to confusion or invented meanings that don't even exist.

The bottom line is everything you've learned so far about the importance and power of words has surely piqued your interest, but how can you tap into this power right away?

One man—one of the twentieth century's most prolific authors and philosophers—continued the work started thousands of years ago and gave us the tools we need to learn and do anything. Through many years of research and testing, he developed an incredibly simple but effective system that allows *anyone* to experience the true power of words. His name was L. Ron Hubbard.

In the 1920s, L. Ron Hubbard's concern for education took root when he realized the "influence of a mislearned word on a life." At that time, he was teaching English in a school in Guam.

He stressed two significant points: first, he wished his students to appreciate the scope of the world beyond their shores; and second, he wanted them to understand how literacy held the key to participation in that world.

During the Second World War, he became involved in the direct instruction of military personnel as well as the redrafting of instructional materials. In a preliminary note on his navigational text, he advised, "Failure to learn definitions results in a later inability to understand explanations, which include those definitions. Easily the most important factor in any study is a comprehension of what is

meant by certain words."

Mr. Hubbard later wrote a great essay on how to use dictionaries to learn words. As you probably know, a dictionary is simply a book about words. *Diction* comes from the Latin word meaning "a word or to say"; *-ary* means "a collection of or a thing connected with."

Here's the essay…

"A dictionary tells a person how to say a word, what it means, how to spell it and how to use it. Dictionaries usually will tell you where a word comes from.

"Definitions (explanations of what the words mean) in dictionaries are not always complete and in some cases are not totally correct. Remember that dictionaries are written by people who themselves might have misunderstood words. So do not treat them as religious texts which must be believed. They are mostly correct but they are just tools.

"A misunderstood word will remain misunderstood until one 'clears' the meaning of the word. Once the word is fully understood, it is said to be 'cleared.' The procedures used to locate and clear up words one has misunderstood in his studies are called Word Clearing. There are several different methods of Word Clearing which will be covered later in this book. The first thing to learn is the exact procedure to be used in clearing any word or symbol one comes across in reading or studying that he does not understand.

"THE ALPHABET

"Knowledge of the alphabet is the key to finding words quickly. To use a dictionary rapidly, one has to be able to recite the alphabet rapidly and know the relations of letters in the alphabet one to the other instantly. Otherwise, one can get lost and it will take a long time to look up words. One literally has to know the alphabet backwards and forwards.

"Words are arranged in alphabetical order in all dictionaries. A dictionary has a section for each letter of the alphabet. The first letter of the word one is looking up tells one which section of the dictionary to look in. Within any section, words are further arranged alphabetically by their second letters, then their third letters and so on. For instance, the word *cat* would be found after the word *castle* and before the word *catch*.

"GUIDE WORDS

"At the top of each page of the dictionary, there are words printed in black heavy type. They are called *guide words*. Guide words show the first and the last words printed on that page or in that column. The page of the dictionary one wants can be found by looking at the guide words on each page. Guide words help find the word being looked for faster.

"PRONUNCIATION

"Pronunciation means the way something is said. A dictionary tells one how to pronounce a word. The pronunciation of a word is given in the dictionary right after the word itself and is usually in parentheses.

"Pronunciation is shown by:

"a. How the word is divided into syllables (a syllable is a word or a small part of a word which can be pronounced with a single, uninterrupted sounding of the voice).

"For example, the word *elephant* contains three syllables:

"cl c phant

"b. How the word, if it has two or more syllables, is accented (the emphasizing of one syllable of a word more than another).

"el' e phant

"The accent mark tells one that the first syllable of the word is the one that is said with emphasis when pronouncing it.

"c. How the individual letters in a word sound through use of a pronunciation key.

"el ə fənt

"Dictionaries use letters and special marks to show how a word sounds. Generally, there are pronunciation keys at the bottom of each page or every other page which list out the most important letters and marks.

"There is also a complete listing near the front which gives the use of every letter or mark used in that dictionary to show how to pronounce a word. By looking at the letters and/or marks in parentheses and checking the pronunciation key at the bottom of the page (or near the front of the dictionary), one learns how the word is pronounced. For instance, to learn how the first 'e' of elephant is pronounced, one looks at the key and sees that it is pronounced in the same way as the 'e' in the words *met* and *rest*. Pronunciation keys differ a bit from dictionary to dictionary but they are all used as described here.

"PARTS OF SPEECH

"Following the pronunciation, the dictionary gives an abbreviation which designates the word's *part of speech*. The parts of speech are the different things words do, such as name a person, place or thing (*noun*), show action or state of being (*verb*), modify or describe another word (*adjective* or *adverb*), etc. This helps you to understand how that word is used in speech and writing.

"When the plural form of a word is made differently than by adding –*s* or –*es* to the singular, the dictionary also includes the plural form of the word, directly after the part of speech.

"For example, the entry for *mouse* in most dictionaries would look similar to this:

"**mouse** (mows) *n.* (*pl.* **mice**)

"DEFINITIONS

"Next comes the definition of the word. If it has more than one definition, most dictionaries number them.

"Often dictionaries give examples showing the use of the word. But in clearing a word, it is not enough for the person simply to read these examples. He has to make up several of his own before he really knows the word.

"Dictionaries also often give specialized definitions when the word has a special meaning in such subjects as law, sports, science, music and so on. They often give slang (words or phrases that are not considered to be 'standard' in the language) definitions for words.

"IDIOMS

"An idiom is a phrase or expression that has a meaning different from what the words suggest in their usual meaning. For example, *to catch one's eye* is an idiom which means *to get one's attention*.

"Most dictionaries include the idioms of a word after the definitions.

"DERIVATION

"A word's derivation (a statement of the origin of a word) is put in brackets. The derivation can be very important to one's full understanding of the word. Words get altered through the ages. By seeing the derivation one can find out what the word originally meant. The word's derivation is usually found at the beginning or the end of the definitions in the dictionary.

"In the derivation certain signs and abbreviations are used.

"The sign < means *derived from*.

"The sign + means *and*.

"The word or words it comes from are written in italics.

Usually abbreviations are used to show the language the word comes from. For example, OE would mean Old English, which denotes the English spoken up to approximately the twelfth century. These abbreviations are defined in the dictionary. Sometimes at the end of the derivation there is a word written in capital letters. This means that further data on the origin of the word can be found under the derivation of the word in capitals.

"EXAMPLE OF A WORD ENTRY

cool (ko͞ol), *adj.*

1. mildly cold; neither warm nor very cold; pleasantly cold:
a cool day.

2. giving a feeling of coolness:
a cool dress.

3. calm; not excited:
to remain cool in spite of trouble.

4. *US Slang.* first rate; superior; admirable:
He drew a cool cartoon.

cool off 1. to calm down. 2. to lose interest.

[Old English *col*, related to COLD]

o͞o as in boot

"DICTIONARY TIPS

"Occasionally, one cannot find a specific word in the dictionary, but by separating a word into its component parts one can look up each part and gain its meaning. Take, for example, the word *antitax.* This word is not defined in most dictionaries, but one can still determine its meaning. One looks up the first part, *anti-,* and finds that it means *opposed to.* One then looks up the second part of the word, *tax,* and finds that it means *money regularly collected from citizens by their rulers.* When one combines the two parts, one gets the definition of *antitax* which means *opposed to collecting of money from citizens by their rulers.*

"Dictionaries sometimes contain lists of such words which are not defined but which can be broken down into their component parts and the meaning determined.

"Words of a special technology require a dictionary composed of terms for that field, e.g., a photographic dictionary or a nautical dictionary.

"To clear a foreign word, get a dictionary of that language. There are two kinds of foreign language dictionaries. One is a dictionary entirely in the foreign language. The other is half in the language the person speaks and half in the foreign language. For instance, in an English/Swedish dictionary, half of the dictionary is English with Swedish words next to it, and the other half is Swedish with its English counterpart next to it. One would use the all-foreign dictionary only when the person being word cleared knew that language fluently.

"Dictionaries contain a lot of information. The format of individual dictionaries varies one to the next but the above fundamentals apply to them all. Dictionaries contain sections in the front which explain how they are used. If one encounters a word, symbol or abbreviation in the entry of a word that he does not understand he can always turn to this introduction section for help."

Not all dictionaries are equal, however. Current dictionaries vary in accuracy and usefulness. Many of these modern dictionaries are virtually worthless and can actually confuse you due to their inaccurate and omitted definitions.

Studying with the wrong dictionary is like trying to play the piano with boxing gloves. Studying with the right dictionary, however, is as easy as breathing.

And there's incredible freedom in study. Wonder why? In the next chapter, you're going to read an inspiring story that will show you how much power words can give you over your life . . . .

Chapter Five

WORDS CAN SET YOU FREE?

"Education is the passport to the future, for tomorrow belongs to those who prepare for it today."
—Malcolm X, public speaker, human rights activist and deeply influential African American

"If we don't do something real soon, I think you'll have to agree that we're going to be forced either to use the ballot or the bullet. It's one or the other in 1964. It isn't that time is running out—time has run out!"

Those words were the beginning of a speech that is remembered as one of the greatest of all time: Malcolm X's "The Ballot or the Bullet" speech of 1964. In this famous speech, Malcolm advised African Americans to cast their votes judiciously, and ultimately, if they couldn't achieve equality through government, to take up arms.

Malcolm Little, commonly known as Malcolm X, will forever have his place in history as one of the most influential African Americans that ever lived. His advocates praised him for indicting white America in the harshest terms for its crimes against black Americans, and his critics accused him of preaching violence and racism. But nobody could deny this fact: his words were so moving and powerful that they opened the eyes and minds of millions.

But how did Malcolm learn to harness the power of words? How did he go from a high-school dropout turned street thug to one of the most important figures in African American history?

Here's the fascinating story of how Malcolm's transformation and journey into history started with a *dictionary*:

Malcolm dropped out of school in the eighth grade after his teacher told him that his goal of becoming a lawyer wasn't realistic as a black man. By the time he was 13, he had lost both of his parents—his father had died and his mother had a nervous breakdown and was institutionalized.

In 1943, Malcolm was 18 and living in Harlem. He was involved in drug dealing, gambling, racketeering, robbery and prostitution. Two years later, he was involved in elaborate burglaries of residences of wealthy, white families. He was arrested for larceny and breaking and entering in 1946 and was sentenced to spend eight to ten years in Massachusetts State Prison.

He was 21 years old and could barely read. "Every book I picked up had few sentences which didn't contain anywhere from one to nearly all of the words that might have been in Chinese," he wrote. He simply skipped the words he didn't know and had little understanding of what the books were actually saying.

He met a self-educated man in prison by the name of John Elton Bembry, a well-regarded prisoner. Malcolm would later describe him as "the first man I had ever seen command total respect…with words." The two became friends and Malcolm decided to educate himself as Bembry had.

Painfully aware of his illiteracy, Malcolm got his hands on a dictionary and began copying every entry—it took a day just to do the first page. Every day, he would copy out a new page and then read aloud each word and its definitions. Slowly but surely, he began to remember them and what they meant. He realized that a dictionary is really a "little encyclopedia" that taught him about people, animals, places, history, philosophy and science.

As his vocabulary grew, so did his understanding of life and the world around him. He found that he could pick up a book "and now begin to understand what the book was saying." He said that "from then until I left that prison, in every free moment I had, if I was not reading in the library, I was reading in my bunk. You couldn't have gotten me out of a book with a wedge."

He preferred to read in his cell, and after "lights out" at ten o'clock, he would sit on the floor by the door and continue his reading under the faint light of the bulb outside his cell. The guards would come around once every hour, and when he heard their footsteps approaching, he would rush back to his bunk and pretend to be asleep. As soon as they had gone, he would be back by the door reading. This would continue until three or four every morning. He said that "three or four hours of sleep a night was enough for me. Often in the years in the streets I had slept less than that."

Malcolm read and read and read. He devoured books on history and was astounded at the knowledge he obtained about the history of black civilizations. He read books by Gandhi on the struggle in India, he read about African colonization and China's Opium Wars. He read about genetics and philosophy. He read about religion.

"Ten guards and the warden couldn't have torn me out of those books. I have often reflected upon the new vistas that reading opened to me. I knew right there in prison that reading had changed forever the course of my life," he said.

Malcolm was paroled and released from prison in 1952. He later reflected on the time he spent in prison: "Months passed without my even thinking about being imprisoned. In fact, up to then, I had never been so truly free in my life."

This new course in life led him to become one of the most prominent figures in the American Civil Rights Movement—something he will forever be remembered for.

Later in his life, one of Malcolm's roles in his organization was that of a teacher. He ran a class for young people where he told them, "Read everything. You never know where you're going to get an idea. We have to learn how to think."

Just before his assassination in 1965, he maintained that one of the things he most regretted in his life was his lack of an academic education. "I would just like to study. I mean ranging study, because

I have a wide-open mind. I'm interested in almost any subject you can mention."

If Malcolm X's story isn't proof of the incredible power words have over your ability to learn and do anything, I don't know what is.

Think about it for a second. By 21, Malcolm's fate seemed to be completely sealed: he was an illiterate, black, drug-dealing pimp stuck in prison, living in the harsh realities of 1940s racism. Where "should" he have gone? He "should've" gone nowhere, of course. His destiny "should've" been a cold, insignificant death in the streets of Harlem. But, using the power of words, he literally re-wrote his destiny in a way that almost defies belief.

So, realize that YOU have the power to make your fate, no matter what your circumstances are. It only depends on your knowledge and actions. As you'll see, what you do with the information in this book can mean the difference between success and failure, happiness and misery, intelligence and stupidity.

Now, remember the idea of conceptual understanding I mentioned earlier? Well, it's time to revisit it, because conceptual understanding is the "open sesame" of your mind. It's what allows you to translate theory into effective action. Without it, studying is about as pointless as giving caviar to an elephant.

How can you ensure you achieve conceptual understanding of anything you study? By the end of the next chapter, you will know.

Chapter Six

THE BEAUTY OF CONCEPTUAL UNDERSTANDING AND HOW TO ACHIEVE IT

"The basic tool for the manipulation of reality is the manipulation of words. If you can control the meaning of words, you can control the people who must use the words."
–Phillip K. Dick, award-winning author of 36 novels

"For me, words are a form of action, capable of influencing change," wrote Ingrid Bengis, an American author and professor. But how much action and change are possible when one doesn't *understand* the words?

Can you remember a time when you were trying to learn something and felt completely confused as to how to actually do it? Well, as you might have guessed by now, the reason why you couldn't understand what to do is you didn't understand words in the material.

Trying to do when you have many misunderstood words is like trying to knock down the Great Wall of China with a hammer. Well, I want to arm you with a crane and wrecking ball. And later, just for good measure, I'm going to give you tools that are the educational equivalent of dynamite: they will allow you to simply blow apart all barriers and obstacles to learning and doing anything.

Now, most people don't know how to gain a conceptual understanding of words—how to "clear" them. To "clear" a word simply means to learn it to full conceptual understanding.

To quote L. Ron Hubbard again, he devised a simple yet powerful system to accomplish this, and here's how you do it:

"1. Have a dictionary to hand while reading so that you can clear any misunderstood word or symbol you come across. A simple but good dictionary can be found that does not itself contain large words within the definitions of the words which have to be cleared.

"2. When you come across a word or symbol that you do not understand, the first thing to do is get a dictionary and look rapidly over the definitions to find the one which applies to the context in which the word was being used. Read that definition and make up sentences using the word that way until you have a clear concept of that meaning of the word. This could require ten or more sentences.

"3. Then clear each of the other definitions of that word, using each one in sentences until you clearly understand each definition.

"When a word has several different definitions, you cannot limit your understanding of the word to one definition only and call the word 'understood.' You must be able to understand the word when, at a later date, it is used in a different way.

"Don't, however, clear the technical or specialized definitions (math, biology, etc.) or obsolete (no longer used) or archaic (ancient and no longer in general use) definitions unless the word is being used that way in the context where it was misunderstood.

"4. The next thing to do is to clear the derivation, which is the explanation of where the word came from originally. This will help you gain a basic understanding of the word.

"5. Most dictionaries give the idioms of a word. An idiom is a phrase or expression whose meaning cannot be understood from the ordinary meanings of the words. For example, *all in* is an English idiom meaning 'very tired.' (In a sentence this might be used, 'Joe did not want to go to the party because he was feeling *all in*.') Quite a few words in English are used in idioms and these are usually given in a dictionary after the definitions of the word itself. If there are idioms for the word that you are clearing, they are cleared as well.

"6. Clear any other information given about the word, such as notes on its usage, synonyms, etc., so you have a full understanding of the word.

"7. If you encounter a misunderstood word or symbol in the definition of a word being cleared, you must clear it right away using this same procedure and then return to the definition you were clearing. (Dictionary symbols and abbreviations are usually given in the front of the dictionary.)

"However, if you find yourself spending a lot of time clearing words within definitions of words, you should get a simpler dictionary. A good dictionary will enable you to clear a word without having to look up a lot of other ones in the process.

"EXAMPLE OF CLEARING A WORD

"Let's say that you are reading the sentence, 'He used to clean chimneys for a living,' and you're not sure what *chimneys* means.

"You find it in the dictionary and look through the definitions for the one that applies. It says 'A flue for the smoke or gases from a fire.'

"You're not sure what *flue* means so you look that up. It says 'A channel or passage for smoke, air or gases.' That fits and makes sense, so you use it in some sentences until you have a clear concept of it.

"*Flue* in this dictionary has other definitions, each of which you would clear and use in sentences.

"Next, read the derivation the dictionary gives for the word *flue*.

"Now go back to *chimney*. The definition, 'A flue for the smoke or gases from a fire,' now makes sense, so you use it in sentences until you have a concept of it.

"You then clear the other definitions. If the dictionary you are using has specialized or obsolete definitions, you would skip them as they aren't in common usage.

"Now clear up the derivation of the word. You find that *chimney* originally came from the Greek word *kaminos,* which means 'furnace.'

"If the word had any notes about its use, synonyms or idioms, they would all be cleared too.

"That would be the end of clearing *chimney.*

"The above is the way a word should be cleared.

"When words are understood, communication can take place, and with communication any given subject can be understood.

"SIMPLE WORDS

"You might suppose at once that it is the BIG words or the technical words which are most misunderstood.

"This is NOT the case.

"On actual test, it was English simple words and NOT technical words which prevented understanding.

"Words like 'a,' 'the,' 'exist,' 'such' and other 'everybody knows' words show up with great frequency as being misunderstood.

"It takes a BIG dictionary to define these simple words fully. This is another oddity. The small dictionaries also suppose everybody knows.

"It is almost incredible to see that a university graduate has gone through years and years of study of complex subjects and yet does not know what 'or' or 'by' or 'an' means. It has to be seen to be believed. Yet when cleaned up his whole education turns from a solid mass of question marks to a clean useful view.

"A test of schoolchildren in Johannesburg once showed that intelligence DECREASED with each new year of school!

"The answer to the puzzle was simply that each year they added a few dozen more crushing misunderstood words onto an already confused vocabulary that no one ever got them to look up.

"Stupidity *is* the effect of misunderstood words.

"In those areas which give man the most trouble, you will find the most alteration of fact, the most confused and conflicting ideas and of course the greatest number of misunderstood words. Take 'economics' for example.

"The subject of psychology began its texts by saying they did not know what the word means. So the subject itself never arrived. Professor Wundt of Leipzig University in 1879 perverted the term. It really means just a 'study (*ology*) of the soul (*psyche*).' But Wundt, working under the eye of Bismarck, the greatest of German military fascists, at the height of German war ambitions, had to deny man had a soul. So there went the whole subject! Men were thereafter animals (it is all right to kill animals) and man had no soul, so the word psychology could no longer be defined.

"THE EARLIEST MISUNDERSTOOD WORD IN A SUBJECT IS A KEY TO LATER MISUNDERSTOOD WORDS IN THAT SUBJECT.

"In studying a foreign language it is often found that the grammar words of one's *own* language that tell about the grammar in the foreign language are basic to not being able to learn the foreign language."

In the next chapter, I'm going to take you back to ancient Rome to learn the secret behind a man not only considered one of its greatest speakers, but one of its most versatile minds.

His name was Marcus Cicero, and he is going to help shed light on the "enlightening power of words."

Chapter Seven

CICERO'S SECRET

"Words for a distinguished style are impossible without having produced and shaped the thoughts, and no thought can shine clearly without the enlightening power of words."
–Marcus Cicero, Roman philosopher, lawyer and one of Rome's greatest speakers

Marcus Tullius Cicero (106 BC – 43 BC) was a Roman philosopher, lawyer, political theorist, and constitutionalist. Cicero is widely considered one of Rome's greatest speakers; he introduced the Romans to the chief schools of Greek philosophy and also created a Latin philosophical vocabulary.

Cicero, famous for his ability to communicate and persuade, knew well of the power of words and had an incredible ability to put this power to work for him. Here's how he put it:

"Words for a distinguished style are impossible without having produced and shaped the thoughts, and no thought can shine clearly without the enlightening power of words."

That quote may seem a bit confusing at first, so let me help. Let's start with the meaning of a word. According to the *New Oxford American Dictionary*, "distinguished" means "successful, authoritative, and deserving great respect." I think it's safe to say these are qualities we would all like to have. And if you are to follow Cicero's advice, how can you achieve them?

Well, you must first produce and shape the thoughts that lead to your success, authority, and respect. What kind of thoughts would lead you to effective action that will make you successful and respected as an expert?

Just think about it for a second, because it applies to every area of your life.

To make more money in your business, for example, you must first form effective thoughts about how to create, package, present, and sell your products and services. You can then put them into action and reap the benefits.

To make your marriage more successful, you must first form effective thoughts about how to improve relations with your spouse, which might involve better communication, a deeper sense of compassion, increased creativity, more romance, and so on.

This even applies to more trivial things like hobbies. Let's say you're trying to learn how to play the piano. To improve, you must first form effective thoughts about how to improve your dexterity, how to better read music, how to create harmonious compositions, and so forth.

The fact is your effective or ineffective actions are always preceded by effective or ineffective thoughts. Every dream of yours and every area or activity you want to succeed in will require correct actions, and every correct action requires the correct thoughts that set it up. And those thoughts are intimately connected with *words*. Words you hear. Words you read. Words you use.

This goes beyond the power of "visualization": this is the core of finding brilliant solutions, of formulating and executing winning strategies, of cultivating your talents and skills.

So how can we experience the "enlightening power of words" and form spot-on, effective thoughts that can be immediately put into action and get real results?

I'm going to make a very bold statement here, but I can back it up with rock-solid proof.

The real secret to achieving your dreams is harnessing the power of words in those areas you want to excel in.

And I'm not talking about hypnosis, programming your brain, the "Law of Attraction," or any other method of "mental manipulation." I'm talking in very real, practical, "why didn't I think of that?" terms.

And the proof? Well, you'll just have to continue reading, because by the end of this book, you'll have no questions as to the validity of that statement.

But right now, I want to give you another tool that you can use to unlock the "enlightening power of words," as Cicero put it.

Imagine you're studying something important—something you want to immediately apply and get results with. Little do you know, you've already passed a slew of misunderstood words and what you *think* the text is saying is not what it's saying. You're sinking in a pit of misunderstood words and you don't even know it.

How can you escape?

Chapter Eight

ESCAPING THE QUICKSAND OF MISUNDERSTOOD WORDS

"For words are magical formulae. They leave finger marks behind on the brain, which in the twinkling of an eye become the footprints of history."
—Franz Kafka, one of the most influential writers of the twentieth century

Picture yourself as Indiana Jones running through a jungle. You're on your way to the ruins of yet another ancient city where priceless treasures await and . . . stop! You've just accidentally leapt into a pit of quicksand! You are slowly sinking. What are you going to do?

Most people would panic and wildly flail their arms, causing themselves to sink even faster. But not you. You know quicksand isn't as dangerous as people think, so long as you know how to escape. You slowly wiggle your legs, carefully spread your arms, and lean back, allowing yourself to float to the top. A few minutes later, you're free and back on your way.

When you're studying, the quicksand pits are filled with misunderstood words, and when mishandled, they cause just as many problems. Skimming over misunderstood words (not clearing them) is like falling into a pit and thrashing—it only makes you sink deeper. To make matters worse, because it's invisible quicksand, unless you know what I'm about to show you, you don't even know you're sinking until it's too late.

Believe it or not, actual mental and physical reactions occur when you go past words you don't understand. I know, it sounds too good to be true. How could it be that simple?

Well, *why* these reactions occur and why clearing words handles them would require a book all on its own to fully explain. L. Ron Hubbard discovered these phenomena during years of intensive research in the field of study, and you will soon experience them for yourself. And ultimately, isn't workability all that matters? You may not know why gravity exists, but you know things that go up must come down.

By spotting these physical reactions, you will immediately know you've gone past a misunderstood word or words. You will then use a simple method to locate the exact word(s) not understood so you can clear them.

Now stop and hear this: these two skills—detecting when you have passed misunderstood words and locating them—are the two most *crucial* skills you can have when learning. Trying to learn without these skills can be like trying to drain a swimming pool with a soda straw—overwhelming, and even if you try, painfully slow.

So, let's look at these physical reactions. Here's what L. Ron Hubbard found in his research:

"Reading on past a word that was not understood gives one...

- "A distinctly **blank feeling**;

- "A **washed-out feeling**;

- "A **'not there' feeling**;

- "And a **sort of nervous hysteria** can follow that.

- "When someone misses understanding a word, the section right after that word is a **blank in his memory**.

"The confusion or inability to grasp or learn comes AFTER a word that the person did not have defined and understood.

"A misunderstood definition or a not-comprehended definition or an undefined word can even cause a person to give up studying a subject and leave a course or class. Leaving in this way is called a 'blow.'"

How could a misunderstood word possibly cause one to quit studying? Well, how fun is it to sit with a book feeling confused, blank, washed-out, not there, and nervous? Is that an activity you would sign up for? Didn't think so.

Most educators don't even recognize the real meaning of these reactions. They slap all kinds of labels on kids who are fidgety and nervous in class ("ADHD"), who "aren't there" and can't concentrate ("ADD"), or who lash out at teachers out of frustration because they don't understand what they're being taught. The sad fact is many of these kids' (and adults' for that matter) "bad" behavior simply comes from a bunch of misunderstood words! We've all experienced this before; I know when I'm full of misunderstood words and am completely confused, I'm very uncomfortable too!

I know this is new territory for you, so it may sound outlandish or impossible, but suspend your disbelief until you've tried it out. From this point on, be alert to any of those reactions. When one appears, it's time to stop studying and find the misunderstood word. How do you do that? I'm glad you asked, because that's the subject of the next chapter.

To ensure your success, I'm going to share with you the surefire way of locating the exact misunderstood word(s) holding you down. Once you've found and cleared them, you will—to your surprise— discover the negative feeling is *gone*. It'll seem like magic. Maybe it is.

When you take these actions, you'll emerge from the quicksand every time. Like Indiana Jones's trusty whip, they will help you casually escape all kinds of danger.

So let's move on. I'm going to reveal to you one divining rod that actually works—the Divining Rod of Learning. (If you're wondering what a "divining rod" even is, you're about to find out . . .)

Chapter Nine

THE ONE DIVINING ROD THAT WORKS

"Thanks to words, we have been able to rise above the brutes; and thanks to words, we have often sunk to the level of the demons."
—Aldous Huxley, author of the famous novel, Brave New World

Since ancient times, a controversial and mystical practice known as *divining* or *dowsing* has existed. This seemingly supernatural technique has allegedly been used to locate hidden sources of underground water, oil, and metals. In the Vietnam War, Marines even tried it to help find enemy weapons and tunnels.

Regardless of whether it works, it's very simple. Using a Y-shaped twig of certain trees and plants or a Y-shaped metal rod, you hold both ends of the "V" (one in each hand) and roam around in the area where you suspect natural treasures are hidden, pointing the tip downward.

As the legend goes, when you pass over the substance you are attempting to locate (water, oil, or metal), the rod's tip will magically rise upward or fall downward all on its own.

While the historical and current effectiveness of the Divining Rod of Water, Oil, and Metal will be endlessly debated, there *is* a simple, 100% workable method to accurately locate misunderstood words when studying, and I'm going to call it The Divining Rod of Learning—and it's a divining rod that works *every time*.

Picture this. You're reading along and notice that you've gone completely blank on what you just read or that you're feeling nervous. You know there's a misunderstood word in there somewhere. You look around for some word you don't fully understand and find nothing. You feel like you're looking for a needle in a haystack.

How do you find the misunderstood word?

There's a very easy and exact way to do it, and it's called the *Basic Word Clearing Procedure*. It was developed by L. Ron Hubbard, and it works like this:

"1. The person is not flying along and is not so 'bright' as he was or he may exhibit just plain lack of enthusiasm or be taking too long on his studies or be yawning or disinterested or doodling or daydreaming, etc.

"2. He must then look earlier in the text for a misunderstood word. There is one always; there are no exceptions. It may be that the misunderstood word is two pages or more back, but it is always earlier in the text than where he is now. The formula is to find out where he wasn't having any trouble and find out where he is now having trouble and the misunderstood word will be in between. It will be at the tag end of where he wasn't having trouble.

"3. The word is found. The person recognizes it in looking back for it. Or, if the person can't find it, one can take words from the text that could be the misunderstood word and ask 'What does_____ mean?' to see if the person gives the correct definition.

"4. The person looks up the word found in a dictionary and clears it (see chapter five). He uses it verbally several times in sentences of his own composition until he has obviously demonstrated he understands the word by the composition of his sentences.

"5. The person now reads the text that contained the misunderstood word. If he is not now 'bright' and eager to get on with it then there is another misunderstood word earlier in the text. This is found by repeating steps 2-5.

"6. When the person is bright and eager to get on with it, he is told to come forward, studying the text from where the misunderstood word was to the area of the subject he did not understand (where step 1 began).

"The person will now be enthusiastic with his study of the subject, and that is the end result of the Basic Word Clearing Procedure. (The result won't be achieved if a misunderstood word was missed or if there is an earlier misunderstood word in the text. If so, repeat steps 2-5.) If the person is now enthusiastic, have him continue with studying.

"Good Word Clearing is a system of backtracking. You have to look earlier than the point where the person became dull or confused and you'll find that there's a word that he doesn't understand somewhere before the trouble started. If he doesn't brighten up when the word is found and cleared, there will be a misunderstood word even before that one.

"This will be very clear to you if you understand that IF IT IS NOT RESOLVING, THE THING YOU ARE APPARENTLY HAVING TROUBLE WITH IS NOT THE THING YOU ARE HAVING TROUBLE WITH. Otherwise, it would resolve, wouldn't it?

"Basic Word Clearing Procedure is tremendously effective when done as described herein. So get a good understanding of it and become expert in its use."

Chapter Ten

THE MIND OF WITTGENSTEIN

"The limits of my language are the limits of my mind. All I know is
what I have words for."
—Ludwig Wittgenstein, influential philosopher of the twentieth century

Ludwig Wittgenstein (1889-1951) was an Austrian-British philosopher who worked primarily in logic, the philosophy of mathematics,
of the mind, and of language.

Two of his most famous works, *Tractatus Logico-Philosophicus* and
Philosophical Investigations, are often listed among the top five most important books in twentieth-century philosophy.

Wittgenstein was keenly aware of the power of words and their
role in expanding his mind and abilities, which is clearly evident in
the quote:

> *"The limits of my language are the limits of my mind.*
> *All I know is what I have words for."*

Think about that for a second, because it is quite a profound
statement. The limits of your language are the limits of your mind
. . . All you know is what you have words for . . . .

How could that be? Well, I'm no Wittgenstein, but here's my understanding: words are the primary tool used to express thoughts,
ideas, and concepts. We urgently need them to express what's within

us and to understand the ideas and beliefs of others.

Our understanding of ourselves, of others, and of life itself is a collection of concepts and feelings we either adopted from others or formulated ourselves (or some combination of those). But if our depth of language is shallow, what do you think this will mean for our depth of understanding of the world around us?

Could you imagine what life would be like if you didn't properly understand a single word you heard? How would you connect with others? How would you share your feelings, thoughts, and desires in an understandable fashion? How would you learn anything that couldn't be immediately demonstrated with objects?

It would be an impossible challenge. Life would be an abstract confusion you'd have no connection with. According to Wittgenstein, your mind and knowledge would be severely limited.

Now, could you imagine what life would be like if you could swiftly and accurately express your ideas, feelings, and beliefs about anything to anyone? What if you could fully understand any concept or idea communicated in any area of life or knowledge? What if you could easily learn and do anything you wanted?

Well, if we turn to Wittgenstein again, your mind and knowledge would have no limits: you could expand endlessly.

Sounds pretty incredible, doesn't it? It is, and you can achieve it if you diligently apply what you're learning in this book .

Chapter Eleven

THE HUNT FOR THE GOLDEN DICTIONARY

"Words—so innocent and powerless as they are, as standing in a dictionary, how potent for good and evil they become in the hands of one who knows how to combine them."
–Nathaniel Hawthorne, American novelist

All tasks require tools. The sculptor needs his hammer and chisel. The scientist needs his laboratory. The photographer needs his camera. The genius needs his *dictionary*. The dictionary is your primary tool—it's your trusty compass, and it will guide you on a great many adventures.

I can say with absolute certainty this simple tool has made me more money and brought me more knowledge than anything else— *hands down*. For it has allowed me to unlock wisdom in any field, as it will do for you; it has allowed me to learn and do anything I've set my mind to, as it will for you.

Picture it as a book of magic formulas that allow you to absorb words and then weave the concepts into powerful spells of action and results.

You may not realize it yet, but you are going to become a dictionary buff. Much like a wine connoisseur, you are going to learn to appreciate—and hate—the subtle differences between different dictionaries. Studying with a bad dictionary is *very* annoying, so make sure you take a look at each of the ones you will soon read about.

As you become familiar with them, you'll develop your own

preferences and will eventually discover the one that's perfect for you. It'll be like when you found the perfect mattress or set of golf clubs—it'll just feel good.

I've noticed that when I have the right dictionary, I actually enjoy clearing words. So keep that in mind.

I must admit though, I am on a never-ending hunt for the golden dictionary. That shining, Swiss army knife of a dictionary that contains every word, idiom, and slang usage I need, whose definitions are crystal clear but detailed, and whose derivations are thorough but not overwhelming.

So I haven't found The One yet, but I've found the following list of dictionaries to be very helpful. My personal favorite is the Oxford brand of dictionaries, though some don't have derivations (get one that does). Also, I think it's worth noting that I've found that older editions are usually better . . . so there are literally hundreds of variations to find out there.

The list below was compiled by writer and philosopher L. Ron Hubbard, a man known for his fantastic vocabulary and command of the English language. According to a study of his written works, he had a vocabulary of approximately *152,000 words*. To put this in perspective, the average college graduate's vocabulary is about 20,000 words, so that's quite a feat.

"Webster's New World Dictionary for Young Readers:

"This is a very simple American dictionary. It is available in most bookstores and is published by New World Dictionaries/Simon & Schuster. It is a hardbound volume and does not contain derivations. When using this dictionary, a person must be sure to clear the derivations in a larger dictionary. The definitions in this dictionary are quite good.

"*Oxford American Dictionary:*

"This is a very good American dictionary, simpler than the college dictionaries yet more advanced than the beginning dictionary listed above. It does not list derivations of the words.

"It is quite an excellent dictionary and very popular with people who want to use an intermediate dictionary.

"It is published in paperback by Avon Books and in hardback by the Oxford University Press.

"*Webster's New World Dictionary of the American Language, Student Edition:*

"This is an intermediate-level American dictionary which includes derivations. It is published by New World Dictionaries/Simon & Schuster and is available in most bookstores.

"*The Random House College Dictionary:*

"This is a college dictionary and somewhat tougher than the dictionaries listed above. This is a one-volume American dictionary published in the US by Random House, Inc., and in Canada by Random House of Canada, Limited.

"This Random House dictionary contains a large number of slang definitions and idioms and also gives good derivations.

"*The Webster's New World Dictionary of the American Language, College Edition:*

"This is an American college dictionary published by New World Dictionaries/Simon & Schuster. It is a one-volume dictionary and gives most of the slang definitions and idioms. It also has good derivations.

"The Concise Oxford Dictionary:

"This is a very concise English dictionary but is not a simple or beginner's dictionary. It is a small, one-volume dictionary. It uses a lot of abbreviations which may take some getting used to, but once the abbreviations are mastered people find this dictionary as easy to use as any other similar dictionary. It is less complicated in its definitions than the usual college dictionary and has the added benefit that the definitions given are well stated—in other words, it does not give the same definition reworded into several different definitions, the way some dictionaries do.

"This dictionary is printed in Great Britain and the United States by the Oxford University Press.

"The Shorter Oxford English Dictionary:

"This is a two-volume English dictionary and is a shorter version of *The Oxford English Dictionary*. It is quite up-to-date and is an ideal dictionary for fairly literate people. Even if not used regularly, it makes a very good reference dictionary. The definitions given in the Oxford dictionaries are usually more accurate and give a better idea of the meaning of the word than any other dictionary.

"This Oxford dictionary is also printed by the Oxford University Press.

"The Oxford English Dictionary:

"This is by far the largest English dictionary and is actually the principal dictionary of the English language. It consists of twenty volumes. (There is a *Compact Edition of the Oxford English Dictionary* in which the exact text of *The Oxford English Dictionary* is duplicated in very small print which is read through a magnifying glass. Reduced in this manner the whole thing fits into two volumes.)

"For many this dictionary may be too comprehensive to use on a regular basis. (For some, huge dictionaries can be confusing as the words they use in their definitions are often too big or too rare and make one chase through twenty new words to get the meaning of the original.)

"Although many people will not use this as their only dictionary, it will be found useful in clearing certain words, verifying data from other dictionaries, etc. It is a valuable reference dictionary and is sometimes the only dictionary that correctly defines a particular word.

"These Oxfords are also printed by the Oxford University Press. If your local bookstore does not stock them, they will be able to order them for you.

"From the dictionaries recommended here, a person should be able to find one that suits him.

"DINKY DICTIONARIES

"'Dinky dictionaries' are the kind you can fit in your pocket. They are usually paperback and sold at magazine counters in drugstores and grocery stores.

"In learning the meaning of words, small dictionaries are very often a greater liability than they are a help.

"The meanings they give are often circular: Like 'CAT: An Animal.' 'ANIMAL: A Cat.' They do not give enough meaning to escape the circle.

"The meanings given are often inadequate to get a real concept of the word.

"The words are too few and even common words are often missing.

"Little pocketbook dictionaries may have their uses for traveling and reading newspapers, but they do get people in trouble. People have been seen to find a word in them and then look around in total confusion. For the dinky dictionary did not give the full meaning or the second meaning they really needed.

"So the dinky dictionary may fit in your pocket but not in your mind.

"Don't use a dinky dictionary.

"DICTIONARIES AND A PERSON'S OWN LANGUAGE

"English dictionaries and American dictionaries differ in some of their definitions, as the Americans (USA) and the English (Britain) define some words differently.

"An English dictionary will have different applications of words that are specifically *English* (British). These usages won't necessarily be found in American dictionaries, as they are not part of the *American* English language. Different dictionaries have things in them which are unique to that language.

"*The Oxford English Dictionary* is a good example of an English dictionary for the English.

"For the most part a person's dictionary should correspond to his own language. This does not mean that an American shouldn't use a British dictionary (or vice versa), but if he does, he should be aware of the above and check words in a dictionary of his own language as needed.

"FALSE AND OMITTED DEFINITIONS

"It has been found that some dictionaries leave out definitions and may even contain false definitions. If, when using a dictionary, a person comes across what he suspects to be a false definition, there is a handling that can be done. The first thing would be to ensure that there are no misunderstoods and then he should consult another dictionary and check its definition for the word being cleared. This may require more than one dictionary. In this way any false definitions can be resolved.

"Other dictionaries, encyclopedias and textbooks should be on hand for reference.

"If a person runs into an omitted definition or a suspected omitted definition, then other dictionaries or reference books should be consulted and the omitted definition found and cleared.

"DERIVATIONS

"A derivation is a statement of the origin of a word.

"Words *originated* somewhere and meant something originally. Through the ages they have sometimes become altered in meaning.

"Derivations are important in getting a full understanding of words. By understanding the origin of a word, you will have a far greater grasp of the concept of that word.

"A person must always clear the derivation of any word he looks up.

"It will commonly be found that a person does not know how to read the derivations of the words in most dictionaries. The most common error they make is not understanding that when there is a word in the derivation which is fully capitalized it means that that word appears elsewhere in the dictionary and probably contains more information about the derivation.

"(For example, the derivation of 'thermometer' is given in one dictionary as 'THERMO + METER'. Looking at the derivation of 'thermo' it says it is from the Greek word *therme*, meaning *heat*. And the derivation of 'meter' is given as coming from the French *metre*, which is from the Latin 'metrum', which is itself from the Greek *metron* meaning *measure*.) By understanding and using these fully capitalized words, one can get a full picture of a word's derivation.

"If someone has trouble with derivations, it is most likely because of the above plus a misunderstood word or symbol in the derivation. These points can be cleared up quite easily where they are giving difficulty.

"An excellent dictionary of derivations is *The Oxford Dictionary of English Etymology*, also printed by the Oxford University Press."

An interesting example of how derivations can help you better understand a word is the derivation of the word "study." The derivation of "study" can be traced back to the Latin *studium*, which meant "study, application," and originally meant "eagerness." It ultimately came from the Latin *studere*, which meant "to work hard and devote oneself."

Do you see how that helps your understanding? To "study" didn't just mean *to read*. It implied hard work, eagerness, devotion, and application of knowledge.

And last but not least, here's a good tip on finding great dictionaries. The large bookstore chains just carry the newest editions, but privately owned stores (and sometimes smaller chains) often carry older editions of dictionaries. I usually find older editions better as they tend to have clearer, more complete definitions, and better derivations.

Another great option is an electronic dictionary. Electronic dictionaries are great, though some people prefer having an actual book. Although the devices themselves are fast and useful, I have two gripes: the dictionaries most devices are loaded with are lacking in definition clarity, and most don't have derivations. But I've found a few that I like in particular, and you can find links to them at http://www.strangepowerofwords.com in our store. You'll also find other dictionaries we've "approved," so I suggest you take a look.

Regardless of whether you want to go with paper or with digital, once you're in front of some dictionaries, look at how each defines a specific word, the derivations each includes, what idioms each lists, and the like.

You will end up preferring one. And who knows, you may even find the Golden Dictionary (and write me if you do!).

So, it's time to get prepared for your adventures. Go to a local bookstore or go online and get a dictionary.

Yes, right now!

Chapter Twelve

THE TEN WAYS YOU CAN
MISUNDERSTAND A WORD

**"Words do two major things: They provide food for the mind and
create light for understanding and awareness."**
–Jim Rohn, famous "Business Philosopher"

"*Ten* ways to misunderstand a word," you say? Yes!

A misunderstood word isn't a simple, black and white thing (what
in life is, right?). It's not as simple as knowing the word or having no
clue what it means.

As you know, there is only one way you can really know a word—
conceptual understanding—but what you didn't know is there are ten
ways you can NOT know a word, and each one is equally important
and problematic.

These ten ways were outlined by L. Ron Hubbard, and here's
what he wrote:

"'MIS-UNDERSTOOD' or 'NOT-UNDERSTOOD' are terms
used to define any error or omission in comprehension of a word,
concept, symbol or status.

"Most people go around thinking that a misunderstood is just
something they obviously don't know—a 'not-understood.'

"A 'not-understood' is a misunderstood, but there are additional
ways a person can misunderstand a word.

"A MISUNDERSTOOD *WORD* OR SYMBOL IS DEFINED AS A WORD OR SYMBOL FOR WHICH THE PERSON HAS:

"1. *A FALSE (TOTALLY WRONG) DEFINITION:* A definition that has no relationship to the actual meaning of the word or symbol whatsoever.

"*Example:* The person reads or hears the word 'cat' and thinks that 'cat' means 'box.' You can't get more wrong.

"*Example:* A person sees an equal sign (=) and thinks it means to subtract something twice.

"2. *AN INVENTED DEFINITION:* An invented definition is a version of a false definition. The person has made it up himself or has been given an invented definition. Not knowing the actual definition, he invents one for it. This is sometimes difficult to detect because he is certain he knows it; after all, he invented it himself. In such a case he will be certain he knows the definition of the word or symbol.

"*Example:* The person when very young was always called 'a girl' by his pals when he refused to do anything daring. He invents the definition of 'girl' to be 'a cowardly person.'

"*Example:* A person never knew the meaning of the symbol for an exclamation point (!) but seeing it in comic strips as representing swear words invents the definition for it, 'a foul curse,' and regards it accordingly in everything he reads.

"3. *AN INCORRECT DEFINITION:* A definition that is not right but may have some relationship to the word or symbol or be in a similar category.

"*Example:* The person reads or hears the word 'computer' and thinks it is 'typewriter.' This is an incorrect meaning for 'computer' even though a typewriter and a computer are both types of machines.

"*Example:* A person thinks a period (.) after an abbreviation means that you halt in reading at that point.

"4. *AN INCOMPLETE DEFINITION:* A definition that is inadequate.

"*Example:* The person reads the word 'office' and thinks it means 'room.' The definition of the word 'office' is 'the building, room or series of rooms in which the affairs of a business, professional person, branch of government, etc., are carried on.' (Ref: *Webster's New World Dictionary of the American Language, College Edition*) The person's definition is incomplete for the word 'office.'

"*Example:* The person sees an apostrophe (') and knows that it means that something is owned ('s) but does not know that it also is used to show that a letter has been left out of a word. He sees the word 'can't' and immediately tries to figure out who *can* is.

"5. *AN UNSUITABLE DEFINITION:* A definition that does not fit the word as it is used in the context of the sentence one has heard or read.

"*Example:* The person hears the sentence 'I am *dressing* a turkey.' The person's understanding of 'dressing' is 'putting clothes on.' That is *one* definition of 'dressing' but it is an unsuitable definition for the word as it is used in the sentence he has heard. Because he has an unsuitable definition, he thinks someone is putting clothes on a turkey. As a result the sentence he has heard doesn't really make sense to him. The definition of 'dressing' that correctly applies in the sentence he has heard is 'to prepare for use as food, by making ready to cook, or by cooking.' (Ref: *The Oxford English Dictionary*)

"The person will only truly understand what he is hearing when he has fully cleared the word 'dressing' in all its meanings, as he will then also have the definition that correctly applies in the context.

"*Example:* The person sees a dash (–) in the sentence 'I finished numbers 3–7 today.' He thinks a dash is a minus sign, realizes you cannot subtract 7 from 3 and so cannot understand it.

"6. *A HOMONYMIC (one word which has two or more distinctly separate meanings) DEFINITION:* A homonym is a word that is used to designate several different things which have totally different meanings; or a homonym can be one of two or more words that have the same sound, sometimes the same spelling, but differ in meaning.

"*Example:* The person reads the sentence 'I like to box.' The person understands this sentence to mean that someone likes to put things in 'containers.'

"The person has the right meaning for the word 'box,' but he has the wrong word! There is another word 'box' which is being used in the sentence he has just read and means 'to fight with the fists, to engage in boxing.' (Ref: *Oxford American Dictionary*)

"The person has a misunderstood because he has a homonymic definition for the word 'box' and will have to clear the second word 'box' before he understands the sentence.

"*Example:* The person sees a plus sign (+) and as it resembles a cross he thinks it is something religious.

"*Example:* The person hears the word 'period' in the sentence 'It was a disorderly period in history' and knowing that 'period' comes at the end of a sentence and means stop, supposes that the world ended at that point.

"*Example:* Homonymic misunderstoods can also occur when a person does not know the informal or slang usage of a word. The person hears someone on the radio singing 'When my *Honey* walks down the street.' The person thinks 'a thick, sweet, syrupy substance that bees make as food from the nectar of flowers and store in honeycombs' is walking down the street! He doesn't know the informal definition of 'honey' which is 'sweet one; darling; dear: often a term of affectionate address' which is how it is being used in the song. (Ref: *Webster's New World Dictionary of the American Language, College Edition*)

"*7. A SUBSTITUTE (SYNONYM—a word which has a similar but not the same meaning) DEFINITION:* A substitute definition occurs when a person uses a synonym for the definition of a word. A synonym is not a definition. A synonym is a word having a meaning *similar* to that of another word.

"*Example:* The person reads the word 'portly' and thinks the definition of the word is 'fat.' 'Fat' is a synonym for the word 'portly.' The person has a misunderstood because the word 'portly' means 'large and heavy in a dignified and stately way.' (Ref: *Webster's New World Dictionary of the American Language, College Edition*) The person does not have the full meaning of 'portly' if he thinks it just means 'fat.'

"Knowing synonyms for words increases your vocabulary but it does not mean you understand the *meaning* of a word. Learn the full definition for a word as well as its synonyms.

"8. *AN OMITTED (MISSING) DEFINITION:* An omitted definition is a definition of a word that the person is missing or is omitted from the dictionary he is using.

"*Example:* The person hears the line 'The food here is too rich.' This person knows two definitions for the word 'rich.' He knows that 'rich' means 'having much money, land, goods, etc.' and 'wealthy people.' Neither of these definitions make much sense to him in the sentence he has just heard. He cannot understand what food could have to do with having a lot of money.

"Omitted definitions can come about from using dinky dictionaries. If the person had looked up 'rich' in a small paperback dictionary, he would probably still be stuck with his misunderstood. A dinky dictionary probably will not give him the definition he needs. In order to understand the word he would have to get a good-sized dictionary to ensure it gives him the omitted definition which is '(of food) containing a large proportion of fat, butter, eggs or spices, etc.' (Ref: *Oxford American Dictionary*)

"*Example:* The person reads 'He estimated the light at f 5.6.' He can't figure out what this 'f' is, so he looks up 'f' in *The American Heritage Dictionary* and wonders if it is temperature or money or sports for 'foul' or maybe the money 'franc.' The text doesn't refer to France so he can't figure it out. Omitted in *The American Heritage* is the photography definition of 'f' which simply means 'the number which shows the width of the hole the light goes through in the lens.' The moral of this is to have enough dictionaries around.

"*NOTE:* It can occur that an accurate definition for a word is not given in any dictionary, which is an error in the language itself.

"9. *A NO-DEFINITION:* A no-definition is a 'not-understood' word or symbol.

"*Example:* The person reads the sentence 'The business produced no lucre.' No understanding occurs, as he has no definition for 'lucre.' The word means 'riches; money: chiefly a scornful word, as in *filthy lucre.* (Ref: *Webster's New World Dictionary of the American Language, Student Edition*) It isn't that he has the word incorrectly, unsuitably or any other way defined; he has no definition for it at all. He has never looked it up and gotten it defined. Thus he does not understand it. The definition does not exist for him until he looks it up and gets it clearly understood.

"*Example:* The person sees a dot at the end of a word on a printed page and having no definition for 'a period (.)' tends to run all of his sentences together.

"10. *A REJECTED DEFINITION:* A rejected definition is a definition of a word which the person will not accept. The reasons why he will not accept it are usually based on emotional reactions connected with it. The person finds the definition degrading to himself or his friends or group in some imagined way. Although he may have a total misunderstood on the word, he may refuse to have it explained or look it up.

"*Example:* The person refuses to look up the word 'mathematics.' He doesn't know what it means, he doesn't want to know what it means, and he won't have anything to do with it. A discussion of why he refuses to look it up discloses that he was expelled from school because he flunked with violence his first month of his first course in mathematics. If he were to realize that he flunked because he didn't know what he was supposed to study, he would then be willing to look the word up.

"*Example:* The person refuses to look up the definition of asterisk (*). On discussion, it turns out that every time he sees an asterisk on the page he knows the material will be 'very hard to read' and is 'literary,' 'difficult' and 'highbrow.'

"Discussion of why he won't look it up usually reveals and releases the negative emotions connected with it which he may never have looked at before. Properly handled, he will now want to look it up, having gained an insight into why he wouldn't.

"Any word you come across which fits one or more of the above definitions of a misunderstood word or symbol must be cleared up, using a good-sized dictionary or more than one dictionary or textbook or encyclopedia."

You may be wondering whether this much detail and discipline is necessary. What's the big deal? Do you *really* need to bother?

Yes. As the saying goes, "the devil is in the details," and if you don't pay close attention to the words you read and the ways you can misunderstand them, you'll risk losing the most powerful benefit of learning—conceptual understanding.

Chapter Thirteen

YOUR JOURNEY BEGINS HERE

"The purpose of words is to convey ideas. When the ideas are
grasped, the words are forgotten."
—Chuang Tzu, influential Chinese philosopher

Think of yourself as Christopher Columbus, about to set out to
find virgin lands. You're assembling your team. You're acquiring your
tools. You're almost ready to set sail, and there's no telling where the
journey will take you. You will learn new things, meet new people,
and witness great wonders. Can you feel the fiery excitement?

Now that you know how to find and clear misunderstood words,
you should start doing it *right away*. Begin your journey to knowledge,
competence, and success.

Aristotle once said, "We are what we repeatedly do. Excellence,
then, is not an act, but a habit." From this point on in the book—and
in anything else you're studying—you should be actively looking for
words you don't understand as you read and clear them in the way
you have learned. Make it a habit, and you'll be well on your way to
excellence.

Word by word, you'll better understand the materials, you'll increase your intelligence and vocabulary, you'll understand things conceptually, and you'll therefore be able to act immediately. You'll even
physically feel better. Don't wait. Decide to start *right now*.

Chapter Fourteen

COMPLETING THE CIRCLE

"Down in their hearts, wise men know this truth: the only way to help yourself is to help others."
–Elbert Hubbard, influential writer and philosopher

South African industrialist Flora Edwards once said, "In helping others, we shall help ourselves, for whatever good we give out completes the circle and comes back to us."

Some of the greatest figures in history are known for the help they gave others and the positive influence they made on others' lives.

How can you help others—friends, family members, whomever—be able to learn and do anything? Well, you could give them this book, but something you can immediately do is help them find and clear misunderstood words! How do you do that?

If you see someone studying who is experiencing any of the mental or physical reactions of a misunderstood word, interrupt that person and ask how it's going. Regardless of what that person says, you know there's a misunderstood word or words somewhere in there.

You then do the Basic Word Clearing Procedure with him or her. You do it exactly as you've learned it in the chapter entitled "The One Divining Rod That Works" (flip back real quick if you don't remember). You're just applying it to someone else rather than yourself.

The key is you must find the *word or words* that person doesn't understand. You must not explain the materials or give advice on how to understand them because that's actually doing that person a disservice. The only reason he or she doesn't understand it is because the words used to communicate the concepts remain a mystery. You must find and clear the words so that person can come to his or her own understanding.

You *will* find words that person doesn't understand, the reactions will disappear, and he or she *will* understand it better once the misunderstood words are found and cleared.

Try it out and watch people change right in front of your eyes.

Chapter Fifteen

YOUR CHILD CAN BE A GENIUS TOO

"Genius is one percent inspiration and ninety-nine percent perspiration."
—Thomas A. Edison, one of the greatest inventors in history

How would you like to guarantee your child's intelligence and ability to do whatever he or she pleases? If you're like most parents, I should have your attention . . . and I don't think I have to even tell you how to do it, but I'll say it anyway—get your child learning words!

I'll bet you anything that if you do, it won't take long for your little prodigy to start amazing the teachers by earning As with an idle yawn. He'll laugh at exams and wonder what's so "advanced" about "Advanced Placement" classes.

Case in point: I graduated high school at age fifteen with a 4.1 GPA. And to be honest, it was a piece of cake because I was zealous with clearing words I didn't understand. It's not hard to pass tests when you have no confusions about what you're studying and can correctly apply it every time.

There's no mystery. It's as predictable as gravity.

I'm going to teach you a new method of word clearing that can be done with children, foreign and semi-literate people. It's very simple to do, and it helps them conceptually understand whatever they're studying. (Remember, even in a child, conceptual understanding turns into ability to *apply* and *do*.)

Before helping people learn with this method of word clearing, you should give them a simple explanation of why learning words is important and what you're going to do. You can tell them this will help them fully understand their materials and be able to do the actions right away. Make sure to get their agreement first; don't force them!

This method, called *Specialized Reading Aloud Word Clearing*, was developed by L. Ron Hubbard and here's how it works:

"In this method the person is made to read *aloud* to find out what he is doing.

"Another copy of the same text must also be followed by the Word Clearer as the person reads.

"Startling things can be observed.

"The person may omit the word 'is' whenever it occurs. The person doesn't read it. He may have some strange meaning for it like 'Israel' (actual occurrence).

"He may omit 'didn't' each time it occurs and the reason traced to not knowing what the apostrophe is (actual occurrence).

"He may call one word quite another word such as 'stop' for 'happen' or 'green' for 'mean.'

"He may hesitate over certain words.

"The procedure is:

"1. Have him read aloud.

"2. Note each omission or word change or hesitation or frown as he reads and take it up at once.

"3. Correct it by looking it up for him or explaining it to him.

"4. Have him go on reading, noting the next omission, word change or hesitation or frown.

"5. Repeat steps 2 to 4.

"His next actions would be learning how to use a dictionary and look up words.
"Then a simple grammar.
"Even a very backward person can be boosted up to literacy by this method."

This brings us to another method of word clearing I'm going to share with you, and it's incredibly powerful.

It will allow you to immediately jump into *any* subject or activity and rapidly learn it with full conceptual understanding. It can also be used to clean up any subject or activity you've had trouble with, allowing you to succeed in it. It's extremely effective and brutally simple.

Chapter Sixteen

HOW TO RESTORE APTITUDE IN ANY SUBJECT AND THE ABILITY TO DO ANY ACTIVITY

"The last motive in the world for acquiring vocabulary should be to impress. Words should be acquired because we urgently need them—to convey, to reach, to express something within us, and to understand others."
—*Vanna Bonta, award-winning novelist*

Which subjects and activities have you had trouble with in your life?

What have you been unable to learn or do?

What if you had mastered those subjects or activities? Would your life be different? What would you have done with that knowledge and ability? What would you do now?

The final method of word clearing I'm going to show you will not only help you understand any subjects you've tried to learn in the past, but it will also allow you to jump into any new subject or activity and rapidly learn it.

It's like *rocket fuel* for study: when followed up with your other tools, you'll launch your knowledge and skills into orbit so quickly you'll even surprise yourself.

First, let's look at possible candidates for this method of word clearing. New subjects or activities you want to learn are always on the list, but what about failed subjects or activities in your past? Here are some more interesting effects of misunderstood words L. Ron Hubbard found in his research:

- "You can trace back the subject a person is dumb in or any allied subject that got mixed up with it to a misunderstood word."

- "There is some word in the subject that the person who is inept didn't define or understand and that is followed by an inability to act in the field of that subject. If a person didn't have misunderstoods, his talent might or might not be present, but his *doingness* would be present."

- "Whenever a person has a confused idea of something or believes there is some conflict of ideas, it is always true that a misunderstood word exists at the bottom of that confusion."

- "A misunderstood word breeds strange ideas."

Can you think of any subjects or activities in which you feel dumb?

Do you find it hard to take effective action in any area of your life?

Are there any subjects or fields that are confusing to you or that you feel you have strange ideas about?

Well, those subjects, areas, or activities are all ripe for *Key Word Clearing*. Misunderstood words are holding you back in those areas, and now you can do something about it.

As you've probably concluded by now, misunderstood words are pure poison. They are like maggots that feed on your mind, and they've destroyed many. Your number one concern when learning something should be to *keep them out of yours!*

Now, the following steps walk you through Key Word Clearing, and they were developed, once again, by L. Ron Hubbard (as you have guessed by now, he was ardent about helping people learn!). The process is very simple, and here's how he explains this technique:

"Where a person is new on a job or new to a subject or where there has been a goof, these steps are done in the following manner.

"1. The Word Clearer makes a list of the KEY (or most important) words relating to the person's duties or job or the new subject.

"This is made up as a list. The Word Clearer looks up each word in the dictionary and writes down the definitions.

"The list may have as few as three words or as many as twenty or thirty.

"(Example: A bank clerk's key words would be 'bank,' 'clerk,' 'money,' 'cash,' 'drafts,' 'teller,' 'accounts,' 'customer,' etc.)

"(Example: There has just been a goof resulting in an upset. The goof centered around 'radio,' 'repairs,' 'operation,' 'operator,' 'electronics,' etc.)

"2. The Word Clearer, without showing the person the definitions, asks him to define each word.

"3. The Word Clearer checks the definition on his list for *general* correctness—not word for word but meaning.

"4. Any slow or hesitancy or misdefinition is met with having the person look the word up and look up any word in the definition the person does not have a grasp of.

"5. One completes his list.

"6. By then the person has been jarred into looking further by the above actions. The Word Clearer asks, 'What other word relating to your job (or subject or error) didn't you understand?'

"7. Each one mentioned is now defined by looking it up."

So, how do you create key word lists? You can choose from several ways:

• Look up the subject or activity in a large dictionary. On a separate piece of paper, write the new, specialized words you encounter in the definitions. Now look up those words and write the new, specialized words you encounter. Go several links deep in this "chain of words," and you will have gathered quite a few "key" words.

• Look at the article(s) on the subject or activity in an encyclopedia and write the specialized words you find.

• Look at the table of contents of an entry-level textbook on the subject or activity and write the specialized words you find.

• In some textbooks, the beginning of each chapter provides a list of key words for that chapter. Write these too.

These four tips should allow you to build comprehensive lists of key words. Simply use a good dictionary to find the definitions for each word. If the terms are too specialized and aren't in a dictionary, you can find every type of specialized dictionary conceivable online.

You'll know you have a good list when, after clearing the words yourself, you feel you've reached a good, fundamental understanding of the subject or activity. You'll understand the "big picture."

And then don't forget to have someone do the word clearing method with you! Some people forget to actually have someone ask them the meanings of the words because they put the list together themselves. That's okay. As you'll see, you probably won't get them all right the first time! It's okay if you have to clear some of the words again.

As you can imagine, this tool is incredibly powerful, as it allows you to gain a quick, detailed understanding of any subject or activity you can then build upon. Use it.

Chapter Seventeen

THE DEADLY CURSE OF . . .

"The learning and knowledge that we have, is, at the most, but little compared with that of which we are ignorant."
—Plato, influential Greek philosopher, writer and mathematician

I have bad news.

You might be cursed. Yes, a real curse that you won't know about until it's too late. Millions of people suffer from it every day and it works hard to crush its victims' happiness, competence and success. It has ruined many lives and will be around until the end of time.

But its power is deceiving. It has an Achilles heel—a small, fatal weakness—that, when struck, eliminates it forever.

It is the *Curse of Ignorance.*

Now, before you take offense, let me first define "ignorance." "Ignorance" is not the same as "stupidity," as many people think. It actually means "lack of knowledge or education" and "unawareness of something, often of something important." It simply means to *not know.*

Knowing that you don't know is actually the foundation of real knowledge and wisdom because, as you can imagine, the person who thinks he or she knows everything will learn nothing. And let's get real—who can really say they know *everything* there is to know in any field or activity?

Many of history's great thinkers warned us of this crippling curse.

Confucius once wrote, "Real knowledge is to know the extent of one's ignorance."

"To know that we know what we know, and to know that we do not know what we do not know, that is true knowledge," wrote Nicolaus Copernicus, the legendary astronomer whose heliocentric epiphany began the Scientific Revolution.

Plato agreed when he wrote, "The learning and knowledge that we have, is, at the most, but little compared with that of which we are ignorant."

The importance of knowing that you don't know can't be overstated. Can you imagine what our world would be like if Isaac Newton had never questioned our understanding of motion and gravity? If Charles Darwin had assumed there was nothing left to learn about the evolution of our species? If Albert Einstein hadn't embarked on his pioneering journey in physics?

Really . . . stop and think about it for a moment.

As you can see, the false assumption of knowledge or understanding can have quite a profound impact in not only your life but the lives of others, too.

How can you protect yourself against this plight?

I think the answer is obvious, but I want to share an essay from L. Ron Hubbard on the subject to really make it clear. Here it is:

"The first obstacle to learning is the idea that 'one knows it all already.'

"A person who thinks he knows all there is to know about a subject will not be able to learn anything in it.

"Such a person doesn't even know what he doesn't know.

"If you asked him if he was willing to learn about it, he would try to avoid your question. He isn't willing to learn about it because he has the false idea that he knows all about it already.

"As an example, I once took a correspondence course in photography, thinking that I might learn a few more tricks in the subject. I had been a rather successful photographer, having sold many of my photographs to magazines, and some of my work had even been published in geography books. However, once I started the course, I only got as far as the third lesson when I found myself bogging and putting it aside.

"Later, I took another look at this correspondence course I was taking and realized that this same course contained the real basics and fundamentals of the subject of photography that I didn't even know existed in it. I saw that I didn't know even the first fundamental of why photographs were taken in the first place!

"It dawned on me that I had been very arrogant and that I really didn't know all there was to know on the subject of photography, and that there was something there to learn.

"Once I could see this, I buckled down and started to study the course for real. I then finished the next eight lessons in two weeks of part-time study and gained a workable understanding of the subject for the first time. All the knowledge and understanding I had learned from that course would have been denied me if I had not overcome the first obstacle to learning.

"On the subject of learning itself, the first datum to learn and the first obstacle to overcome is: *'Why are you studying it if you know all about it to begin with?'*

"If a person can decide that he does not already know everything about a subject and can say to himself, 'Here is something to study, let's study it,' he can overcome this obstacle and be able to learn it.

"This is a very, very important datum for any person to learn. If he knows this and applies it, the gateway to knowledge is wide open to him."

Now, I want to pat you on the back for everything you've learned so far. This is a lot to take in, and you're doing very well.

Hang in there and keep at it, because little do you know, with each word you clear, you will develop an ability best likened to the

golden touch of King Midas.
    Read on . . .

Chapter Eighteen

THE PHILOSOPHER'S STONE

"The evolution of knowledge is toward simplicity, not complexity."
–L. Ron Hubbard, best-selling author and philosopher

Have you heard of the philosopher's stone? As the story goes, a mythical substance (not an actual stone) existed that could turn inexpensive metals into gold. It was also sometimes believed to be an "elixir of life," granting immortality to anyone who drank it. For a long time, it was the most sought-after goal in Western alchemy.

According to legend, the thirteenth-century scientist and philosopher Albertus Magnus discovered the philosopher's stone and passed it to his student, the great scholar Thomas Aquinas, shortly before his death circa 1280. Magnus doesn't claim he discovered the "stone" in his writings, but he did record that he witnessed the creation of gold by "transmutation" (the conversion of metals into gold).

The puzzle continued through the ages. A mystical text published in the seventeenth century called the *Mutus Liber* ("wordless book") was rumored to be an instruction manual for concocting a philosopher's stone. It was a collection of fifteen illustrations and nothing more.

While we may never solve that mystery, we have already solved a different one. You are holding a philosopher's stone in your hands. The learning technology you now know is the powerful substance that allows you to take cold, lifeless words and transmute them into lively, effective *action* that creates success, money, happiness, and ability.

It is up to you to use it, though. Surely you've heard the old saying, "You can take a horse to water, but you can't make him drink." The eternal spring of knowledge has been revealed to you, but you have to drink from it to benefit.

It takes discipline to find and clear words correctly. Sometimes you'll want to just continue reading. Sometimes you'll be clearing so many words you won't feel like you're making progress in the material itself.

Don't despair. Just keep pushing forward. The payoff for doing it *right*—just as described in this book—is so huge that it's worth it.

Thomas Edison wrote, "The three great essentials to achieve anything worthwhile are, first, hard work; second, stick-to-itiveness; third, common sense." These words came from a man who not only co-founded General Electric and invented the phonograph, the light bulb, and the motion picture camera (with the help of his employee, W.K.L. Dickson), but he also held a world-record number of patents—over 1,000 singly- and jointly-held in all.

So, work hard at this and stick to it. You've probably already concluded that it's a pretty common sense approach to learning.

And as you use these methods, you'll "magically" become a fast student who can take up *anything* and rapidly learn it.

You'll "magically" enjoy studying because of the results you get from it.

You'll "magically" become better at speaking and writing. You'll be more eloquent and convincing.

You'll "magically" become an authority on things within your circles because your friends and family will recognize how well you understand and can do them.

You'll "magically" become more and more interested in learning and doing new things, something others will notice.

You'll "magically" grow your vocabulary. Imagine having such a

large vocabulary that you can properly define almost *every* word used in a book!

In short, anything viewed through your "window" will be conquerable.

Interestingly, these tools will not be found in the mainstream educational system for reasons we won't go into in this book. One can look at the steadily declining results of our educational system and wonder what is really going on. The public education system's solution is to simply lower passing grades, but what does that mean for future generations?

In 2003, a study was done of almost 2,000 university students. National newspapers such as *USA Today* reported on the study, which showed 70 percent of students graduating with two-year degrees couldn't handle simple tasks such as interpreting a table about exercise and blood pressure, understanding the arguments of newspaper editorials, comparing credit card offers with different interest rates and annual fees, or summarizing the results of a survey about parental involvement in school.

How do you think four-year graduates did?

Fifty percent of them had the same problems.

Almost 20 percent of students pursuing four-year degrees had only basic quantitative skills. For example, the students could not estimate whether their car had enough gas to get to the service station. About 30 percent of two-year students had only basic math skills.

The results of the study were disturbing and shone a spotlight on how utterly ineffective our modern educational methods are.

The learning techniques taught in this book are a big part of the solution. Were you ever taught in school to give any special attention to learning words you didn't understand? Probably not. But isn't that strange? As you've seen, the power of words has been known for thousands of years . . . why isn't that taught to our children?

Who knows. I can tell you this though: misunderstood words are one of the *key* reasons why we are stuck in this Dark Age of Learning Disabilities and why a real understanding of words will pave the road to the Golden Age of Learning Abilities.

The fact is, attempting to learn and retain information without learning words is like trying to catch rain with a spaghetti strainer.

Albert Einstein wrote, "The only thing that interferes with my learning is my education." He also said, "It is a miracle that curiosity survives formal education." So don't let whatever you were taught in school prevent you from trying something new. You have nothing to lose, and everything to gain.

Eventually, if you work hard at it, you will achieve what I'll dub the Holy Grail of Learning.

You will achieve *superliteracy*.

What is it and how will it benefit you?

Turn the page and find out.

Chapter Nineteen

THE HOLY GRAIL OF LEARNING

"Education is not filling a bucket, but lighting a fire."
—William Butler Yeats, Nobel Prize-winning poet

Here it is—the Holy Grail of Learning. It grants limitless power for you to be, do, and have anything, and it can only be obtained by the sweat of your brow. There are no shortcuts. No amount of money or power can buy this priceless jewel.

So, what is it? *Superliteracy.* That term was coined by L. Ron Hubbard, and he wrote an entire article about it. Here is what he wrote:

"SUPER—Superiority in size, quality, number or degree.

"LITERACY—The ability to read and write.

"Almost everyone these days is able to read and write. This was not true a century ago but, with modern stress on education, it is true today.

"But is this enough today?

"It is an instruction-book world. The civilization in which we live is highly technical.

"Education today goes into the twenties.

"That's a third of one's life.

"And what happens when one leaves school?

"Can he *do* what he studied?

"Does he *have* all his education or did it get left behind?

"*Literacy* is not enough.

"Today's schools and today's world require a new ability—the ability to look at a page without any strain and absorb what it says and then apply it right now without any stress at all.

"And is that possible?

"Am I talking about speed reading?

"No. That is just being able to read rapidly. It does not improve the *comfort* of reading and it does not improve the ability to apply. What is really needed is the ability to COMFORTABLY and QUICKLY take data from a page and be able at once to APPLY it.

"Anyone who could do *that* would be SUPERLITERATE.

"What happens?

"The average person—literate—is able to read words and mentally record words.

"Like this:

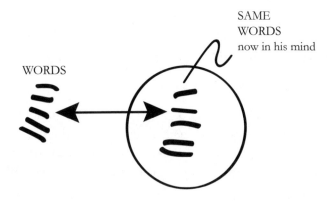

"When he writes he writes:

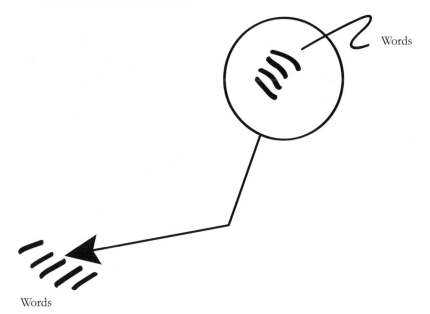

Words

Words

"In his mind words are 'understood' as other words like this:

"When one is superliterate, this is what happens:

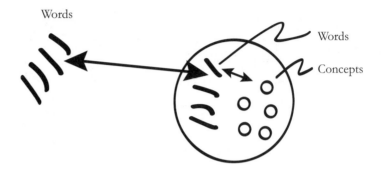

"Therefore as he is dealing in *concepts* (ideas or understandings) this can happen:

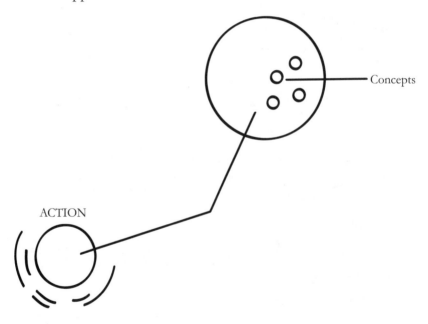

"And he thinks in concepts to which he can fit words easily and so can write clearly.

"In other words, when one is superliterate, one reads not words but understandings. And so one can act.

"The idea of grasping word meanings conceptually is something new to the field of linguistics. The endless semantic circles pursued by Korzybski and company never really led to the realization that a word and its meanings are embodied in the basic *concept* or *idea* symbolized by that word.

"That conceptualization of meanings is foreign to dictionary writers and 'experts' is evidenced by the fact that definitions are so subject to change with the passage of time.

"For example, modern definitions of the word 'understand' are found to be largely inadequate. A really full and meaningful definition of it could only be found in a first edition of *Webster's Dictionary of Synonyms*, 1942.

"*Understand*: To have a clear and true idea or conception, or full and exact knowledge, of something. In general it may be said that *understand* refers to the result of a mental process or processes (a clear and exact idea or notion, or full knowledge). *Understand* implies the power to receive and register a clear and true impression.

"A *CLEARED WORD* is defined as follows:

"A WORD WHICH HAS BEEN CLEARED TO THE POINT OF FULL CONCEPTUAL UNDERSTANDING.

"There are many ways and combinations to achieve this. Using the word in sentences until the meaning is grasped conceptually is the most common."

As you continue to apply the technology you have learned, you will approach this incredible state. Others will notice. They will call you a genius. They will ask how you do it.

You can simply give them this book.

Chapter Twenty

YOUR CHALLENGE

"Without knowing the force of words, it is impossible to know men."
—Confucius, deeply influential Chinese philosopher

I hope you realize the importance of the tools you now possess. With them, you can achieve anything you put your mind to. They really are that powerful, and so are you.

Samuel Johnson, a man considered to be one of the most distinguished authors in English history, once wrote, "If your determination is fixed, I do not counsel you to despair. Few things are impossible to diligence and skill. Great works are performed not by strength, but by perseverance."

It won't be easy to achieve the success you've always dreamed of, it won't be easy. It's going to take intense study and hard work. But never forget the prize at the end.

In 1907, Ernest Shackleton was trying to put together a crew to sail with him on his exploration of the South Pole. He placed an ad in the London *Times* that read: "Wanted. Men for hazardous journey. Low wages. Bitter cold. Long hours of complete darkness. Safe return doubtful. Honor and recognition in the event of success." The next morning, over 5,000 men lined up outside the newspaper's office, hoping to be one of the few chosen for the historic journey.

People are willing to go to hell and back for the right cause. Every great achievement of mankind was spurred on by a genius with this mindset.

As writer and philosopher L. Ron Hubbard said:

"Purpose only becomes real when it gets to the blood, sweat and tears stage, you know? You have to suffer a little bit. If there's no suffering involved at all nobody knows he's experiencing anything.

"Another thing that's quite interesting about such an activity, it always requires a certain amount of sacrifice—always requires a certain amount of sacrifice— whether of time or of personal interest or even personal possessions, some slight degree. A big game always requires some sacrifice."

The tools in this book will keep you on the track, and it's up to you to pour on the coal. If you do it with enough energy and perseverance, though, you are guaranteed success, just as the train is guaranteed to arrive at the station.

The great Albert Einstein said, "Intellectual growth should commence at birth and cease only at death."

So challenge yourself. What have you always wanted to learn or do? What are you doing that you have ceased growing in? Where could you improve? Nothing is too complicated, too large, or out of the question.

What skills would you like to have?

What would you like to know more about?

Just decide. What is most appealing to you right now?

Good, then that's where you will start. Use the tools taught in this book and go learn it and *do* it.

And ignore the naysayers and defeatists. Barbara Grogan, former chairman of the Federal Reserve Bank of Kansas City, commented in *Esquire* magazine that "The world is chock full of negative people ... They have a thousand reasons why your dreams won't work, and they're ready to share them with you at the drop of a hat. Well, this sounds trite, but you just have to believe in yourself and in your

ability to make your dreams come true."

One day, when you've accomplished your goals, when people compliment you and tell you how they envy your success, your lust for knowledge, and your extraordinary ability to apply what you learn, let them join you.

Give them this book.

GLOSSARY

abstract: difficult to understand. Page 54.

Achilles heel: a weakness or vulnerable point. Page 87.

ADD: attention deficit disorder. A label that has been given to those, usually children, with a constant pattern of impulsiveness, a short attention span, and often hyperactivity, which is given as a reason for difficulty with educational, occupational, and social activities. Page 46.

ADHD: attention deficit hyperactivity disorder. A label given to someone, especially a child, who has certain distracted behaviors, such as forgetfulness, not finishing tasks, and not appearing to listen, hyperactivity and impulsive behaviors such as fidgeting or squirming, difficulty remaining seated, excessive running or climbing, feelings of restlessness, difficulty waiting one's turn, interrupting others, and excessive talking—activities considered normal for children in the past. Page 46.

alchemy: a form of chemistry studied in the Middle Ages, which was concerned with trying to discover ways to change ordinary metals into gold. Page 91.

apply: to make use of something to achieve a result. Page 6.

ballot: the process of voting, in writing and typically in secret. Page 29.

biology: the science of living things; study of plant and animal life. Page 34.

Bismarck: Otto von Bismarck (1815-1898), German political leader and first chancellor (chief of government) from 1871-1890. Bismarck was called the "iron chancellor"; he fought wars with Denmark, Austria and France as part of his plans to unify Germany. Page 37.

bogging: being stuck and unable to make progress. Page 89.

brackets: marks ([ ]) used in dictionaries:

a. to enclose additional information or directions, etc. Example: She said "I wuv [love] you."

b. sometimes to enclose examples given in the dictionary. Example: *house* 1. a building in which people live [*They are in their house.*]

c. to enclose the derivation of a word. Example: *pen* [from Old French *penne*, from Latin *penna*, feather]. Page 25.

chock full: filled to the point of overflowing. Page 104.

concept: a thought devoid of (completely without) symbols, pictures, words or sounds. It is the direct idea of something rather than its sound or symbol. *See also* **symbol** *in this glossary*. Page 15.

correspondence course: a course of instruction by mail, given by a school which sends lessons and examinations to a student periodically, and corrects and grades the returned answers. Page 88.

counterpart: a person or thing closely resembling another, especially in function. Page 27.

crushing: overwhelming. Page 36.

dark age: a time during which a civilization undergoes a decline. Page xvi.

definition: a statement of the meaning of a word. Page 12.

deficit: a lack or shortage of something. Page 46.

delve: research intensively into something. Page 6.

denotes: is a mark or sign of; indicates. Page 26.

derived: came from a source or origin; originated. Page 25.

distinctly: to a clear and noticeable degree. Page 44.

distinguished: successful, authoritative and deserving great respect. Page 39.

divining rod: a forked stick used as a device for sensing underground water sources or minerals. The diviner holds an end of the rod in each hand, and the rod is said to move sharply upward or downward when the diviner walks over a water source or minerals. Page 47.

dub: 1. a pool of water; puddle. Page 14.

2. give an unofficial name or nickname to. Page 95.

dull: mentally slow; lacking brightness of mind; somewhat stupid. Page 52.

duplicate: the action of something being made, done or caused to happen again; the action of reproducing something exactly. Page 59.

ə: schwa. An unstressed vowel, e.g. "a" in "above" or "e" in "sicken." It is represented by the symbol **ə**. Page 24.

e.g.: for example; from the Latin words *exempli gratia*. Page 27.

economics: the science concerned with the production and consumption or use of goods and services. Page 37.

elixir: a magical or medicinal potion, especially (in former times) one supposedly able to change metals into gold or prolong life indefinitely. Page 91.

emotion: a strong feeling about somebody or something. Page 15.

encounter: find oneself faced with. Page 27.

epiphany: an illuminating discovery or realization. Page 88.

fascists: people who believe in or practice *fascism*, the principles or methods of a government or a political party favoring rule by a dictator, with strong control of industry and labor by the central government, great restrictions upon the freedoms of individuals, and extreme nationalism and militarism. Page 37.

fluently: spoken or written easily, smoothly and clearly. Page 27.

formulae: plural of formula. Page 43.

furnace: an enclosed chamber in which material can be heated to very high temperatures. Page 36.

golden age: the period when a specified art or activity is at its peak. Page xvi.

GPA: Grade Point Average. The average of a student's grades over a fixed period, calculated by assigning a value of 4 to A, 3 to B, 2 to C, 1 to D, and 0 to F. Page 77.

grammar: the way words are organized into speech and writings so as to convey exact thoughts, ideas and meanings. It is essentially a system of agreements regarding the relationship of words to bring about meaningful communication. Page 37.

grasp: get hold of mentally; understand. Page 12.

harness: to gain control of something and use it for some purpose. Page 29.

heliocentric: the theory that the earth and the other planets move around the sun. Page 88.

herein: in this writing. Page 52.

highbrow: intellectual, academic, often difficult to understand. Page 71.

hyperactivity: a higher than normal level of activity. Hyperactivity can be used to describe the increased action of a body function, such as hormone production, or behavior. Page 46.

hysteria: any outbreak of wild, uncontrolled excitement or feeling, such as laughing and crying. Page 44.

inability: a lack of power or resources to do something. Page 12.

indict: formally accuse or charge (someone) with a serious crime. Page 29.

industrialist: one who owns or controls large industrial companies. Page 75.

industry: the work and processes involved in collecting raw materials and making them into products in factories. Page 75.

italics: letters that slant to the right. Sometimes used in book titles or to show emphasis. *These are italics.* Page 25.

Johannesburg: city in South Africa. Page 36.

key: a thing that explains or solves something else. For example, a book of answers or a set of symbols for pronouncing words. Page 6.

King Midas: In Greek mythology, Midas (the king of ancient Turkey) is popularly remembered for his ability to turn everything he touched into gold. Page 90.

knowledge: general awareness or possession of information, facts, ideas, truths or beliefs gained through experience or education. Page xi.

Korzybski: Alfred Korzybski was a Polish-born American scientist and philosopher best known for his development of general semantics (a philosophical approach to language that explores the relationship between the form of language and its use and the attempt to improve the ability to express ideas). Page 101.

larceny: the unlawful taking and removal of another person's property. Page 30.

learn: gain knowledge of or a skill in something through study, experience, or by being taught. Page xii.

Leipzig: a city in Germany; the location of Leipzig University, where Wilhelm Wundt and others developed "modern" psychology. Page 37.

linguistics: the science of languages, or of the origin and application of words. Page 101.

mathematics: also known as *math*: the study of numbers, quantities, shapes and spaces using special systems of symbols and rules. Page xv.

misunderstand: to fail to realize the real or intended meaning of something, the true nature of something, or what somebody is really like. Page xi.

modifier: a modifier is something that limits, restricts or describes. Adjectives and adverbs are modifiers. For example, "large" in the sentence, "That is a *large* house," is a modifier. Page 24.

mogul: an important or powerful person. Page 1.

nautical: relating to sailors, navigation, or ships. Page 27.

naysayer: a person who habitually expresses negative or pessimistic views. Page 104.

not-comprehended: not grasped mentally; not understood. Page 46.

noun: a word that names the things we are talking about. A noun names a person, place or thing. Page 24.

parentheses: marks [( )] used to put additional information into a statement, a question or a definition. Example: She has the flowers (roses). Page 23.

patent: an exclusive right officially granted by a government to an inventor to make or sell an invention. Page 92.

philosopher: somebody who seeks to understand and explain the principles of existence and reality. Page xii.

phonograph: a record player. Page 92.

pique: to cause a feeling of interest, curiosity, or excitement in somebody. Page 20.

plural: a form of a word which indicates more than one person, place or thing is being talked about. Page 24.

prestigious: having a high reputation; honored; respected. Page 6.

prime minister: the person who holds the position of head of the government in some countries. Page 15.

prodigy: a person, especially a young one, with exceptional abilities. Page 77.

prolific: (of an artist, author, etc.) producing many works. Page 20.

psychology: the scientific study of mental processes and behavior. Page 37.

racketeering: the act of obtaining money by an illegal enterprise usually involving intimidation. Page 30.

redraft: to rewrite something, making changes in it. Page 20.

science: knowledge based on observed facts and tested truths arranged in an orderly system. Page xv.

semantic: having to do with the study of the meanings of words. Page 101.

singular: a form of a word which indicates one person, place or thing is being talked about. Page 24.

study: the reading of books or examination of other materials to gain knowledge. Page 5.

survival of the fittest: a nineteenth century phrase invented by Herbert Spencer (1864) to describe Charles Darwin's theory that only those organisms best adapted to existing conditions are able to survive and reproduce. Page 17.

symbol: something that could represent or stand for a thought or a thing. For example, the red octagon is a symbol for "STOP" in the United States, and the heart is a symbol of love. Page 16.

synonyms: words in the same language that have a similar meaning to another word in that language. Example: *Big* and *large* are *synonyms*. Page 35.

technology: the methods of application of an art or science as opposed to mere knowledge of the science or art itself. Page 11.

thought: an idea, plan or opinion produced by mental activity. Page 13.

to hand: within reach; near; close. Page 34.

transmutation: the conversion of regular metals into gold or silver. Page 91.

trite: repeated too often; lacking originality or freshness. Page 104.

understand: to grasp the meaning of something. Page xi.

university: a high-level educational institution in which students study for degrees and academic research is done. Page 6.

verb: a word or words that show action or state of being. Page 24.

virtually: for the most part; almost wholly; just about. Page 28.

word: a group of letters or sounds which can have more than one meaning. Page xi.

Wundt: Wilhelm Wundt (1832-1920), German psychologist and physiologist (expert in the study of the functions of living things and the ways in which their parts of organs work); the originator of the false doctrine that man is no more than an animal. Page 37.

yet: for all that; nevertheless; but. Page 36.

INDEX

IF YOU'RE READY TO LEARN ANY SUBJECT OR ACTIVITY, WE CAN HELP!

How would you like to get FREE help learning any subject or activity from a Certified Learning Coach?

Businesspeople! Want To Know How to Use The Breakthroughs In This Course to Increase Productivity and Reduce Turnover?

Are your numbers suffering due to lost sales?

Do your employees make costly mistakes that drive you up the wall?

Are the insidious costs of turnover stealing your profits?

Would you like to kick productivity into high gear?

Wouldn't It Be Amazing If You Had an Easy, Powerful Way to Create More Sales, Increase Productivity and Reduce Turnover?

Imagine if you could have your employees do simple, powerful exercises based on the word clearing breakthroughs taught in this course that will improve their ability to sell your products or services, make them better at their jobs and reduce the number of mistakes they make . . . all resulting in high morale and employee retention.

We've developed and delivered these exercises to over 2,000 employees in over 17 different industries, and they *work like magic*. They are beautifully simple but incredibly <u>powerful</u>.

One of our clients had an **immediate 200% increase in sales** by doing nothing more than these exercises with their salespeople!

Another client found that their inability to really penetrate their market was directly caused by the fact that their salespeople had no idea how to "talk the talk" with prospects because they had no idea what all the words meant—something that we fixed, sending their numbers sky-high!

Yet another client discovered that their employees didn't understand

and couldn't explain the meaning of the industry they were in! Can you imagine the problems that was causing?

Free Special Report Will Prove It Beyond The Shadow of a Doubt

If you really want to see the power of word clearing in action, call us today at 1-800-809-0487 or visit us on the Web at **www.strangepowerofwords.com/business** to receive a FREE SPECIAL REPORT on the use of word clearing exercises in the workplace!

Exciting Business Opportunity! What If You Could Make Great Money Helping Others Learn Any Subject or Activity?

Imagine how many people out there need help learning things.

Imagine how many businesses have trouble teaching their employees how to do their jobs.

Imagine how many kids are struggling in school because they don't know how to learn their subjects.

Picture the millions of people whose lives could be helped with this course.

Well . . .

We Have A TURNKEY Business System That You Will Not Only <u>Love</u> To Do, But It Will Also Make You <u>Great Money</u>

You can do this full-time or part-time and <u>really make a difference in people's lives</u>!

This system <u>puts you in business for yourself</u>, is <u>simple</u>, <u>proven</u> and has <u>great income potential</u>. It is also *completely scalable*—it can be as small as just you or as large as you running a 100-man group!

We have everything worked out for you; just give us a call!

E-MAIL US TODAY AT <u>BUSINESS@STRANGEPOW-EROFWORDS.COM</u> TO LEARN MORE ABOUT THIS INCREDIBLE OPPORTUNITY!

www Scientology.org

SEAN CLOUDEN is the co-founder and President of Accelerated Training Solutions, a training company that specializes in helping businesses maximize productivity and reduce turnover. He currently resides in Clearwater, Florida with his wife, Sarah, and is 25 years old.